Unlocking Grace

A Study Guide in the Doctrines of Grace

Roger L. Smalling

Roger Smalling, *Unlocking Grace*
©2001 by Roger Smalling.

Published by Deo Volente Publishing
P.O. Box 4847
Los Alamos, NM 87544

Printed in the United States of America.

Scripture taken from the Holy Bible, New King James Version
Copyright © 1982 by Thomas Nelson, Inc.
Used by permission

ISBN: 0-9658804-8-6

Table
of Contents

Preface

Have you ever wondered why God did not define "grace" right at the beginning of the Bible? Since we are saved by grace, He could have inspired a prophet to begin the Bible with a dictionary definition such as, "grace is. . ." This would be to the point, just as we like it.

Instead, we encounter stories about imperfect people whom God favored for little apparent reason. These stories give a us clues about the meaning of grace, but leave us without a clear definition.

Next we encounter a series of negations. We see in the Bible that grace is not 'works,' that grace is not deserved, that grace is divine rather than human, and so forth. These negations add a little more shape to our definition of grace, but nailing it down seems like grabbing smoke.

Then we notice how the writers of the Bible connected grace with certain teachings they claimed are important. These doctrines quickly begin to unlock the definition, and our understanding improves.

When we encounter the Cross, though, the entire Bible takes on substance. The fog lifts, and the reason for the delay becomes evident.

God could have given us a short definition, but it would be pitifully shallow. The longer route turns out to be deeper and infinitely more satisfying.

Grace itself would never short-change us with paltry

definitions. So God goes about defining grace in the only way that could do it justice. Grace is altogether too glorious to do it any other way. Why? Grace reflects an essential element of God's character. Each member of the Trinity contributes in His own awesome way. Looking at it like that, it seems amazing that the Lord managed to define it at all, since grace is involved with defining Himself.

When we grasp the definition, we declare, "Oh, how remarkably SIMPLE!" Then we do a double-take and proclaim, "But how incredibly PROFOUND!"

After all, that's typical of His style, isn't it? Did we expect anything else?

That's one reason why I believe that the "Doctrines of Grace" are biblical. They are His style. His fingerprints are all over them.

So, the study of grace turns out to be an involved journey, with unexpected twists. One of these twists is that while we are defining grace, we find ourselves defined more clearly — like it or not. The trip is long but not boring, and it is truly exhilarating with glorious scenery along the way.

Different people delight in various aspects of the trip. Some revel in the authority of a Sovereign Will. Others savor the security of an eternal Covenant. Still others will be enthralled at the power of the Cross. Personally, the part of the trip I enjoy the most, is that it lasts forever.

Enjoy the journey.

Introduction

Four hundred years ago, the Protestant Reformation stimulated a "rediscovery" of the Bible and several of its significant doctrines. These doctrines conflicted with the teachings of the time by affirming that salvation is by grace alone with no contribution by man. Consequently, these doctrines became known as "the doctrines of grace."

The controversy continues today. These biblical teachings are so destructive to man's pride that human emotion rebels against them. Sinful humanity imagines itself to be "the captain of its fate," fully able to contribute to its own salvation.

This study of the doctrines of grace was done originally in Spanish by Roger Smalling, a missionary to Latin America. For easier memorization, he used the acronym "Si, Jesus" (Yes, Jesus) to represent the doctines of grace. Each letter of the phrase "Si, Jesus" represents one of these doctrines. The author has chosen to maintain this form in the English version to preserve the acronym and simplify the study of these truths.

Si, Jesus

S: *Sovereignty of God*

The word *sovereign* means "in control of everything." This doctrine teaches that God controls everything that happens and that all reality is a consequence of divine decrees established from eternity before the creation of the world.

I: *Inability of Man*

When Adam fell, humanity lost all ability to contribute to salvation. Sin infects every aspect of individuals and enslaves them. This doctrine also deals with the issue of "free will." It teaches that sinners are incapable of choosing Christ and cannot produce saving faith apart from a miracle of grace. "Total Inability" or "Total Depravity" are other terms frequently used to describe this doctrine.

J: *Justification by Faith Alone*

God requires absolute righteousness from humanity – the righteousness described in His moral Law. How then is it possible to be righteous before God, knowing that we fallen humans cannot keep the Law perfectly? Christ fulfilled the Law's demands as our substitute, both in His life and in His death. When we accept Christ, God not only forgives our sins, but also credits to us the perfect righteousness of Christ. Thus, we have an imputed perfection which meets God's holy demands and forms the basis of our acceptance before God.

E: Election By Grace

Before the foundation of the world, God chose certain individuals as recipients of His saving grace. He did this apart from any foreseen conditions in us. God's choice was not based on His "foreknowledge" that certain people would choose to receive Christ. Actually, no unsaved person can choose to receive Christ since they are dead in sin. Although Election is not based on human merits, it is not arbitrary. This doctrine presents grace as a product of God's sovereign decree in eternity, not as a response to something man thinks or does.

S: Sacrifice of Christ

The sacrifice of Jesus causes the salvation of the elect. The crucifixion made salvation much more than a mere possibility. It *accomplished* salvation for all the elect. Although Christ's sacrifice is sufficient to save everyone, God the Father intended it for His elect only. The cross guarantees that God's chosen ones will believe. This doctrine is also called "Limited Atonement," and "Particular Redemption."

U: Unity and Universality of the Church

The Church of Christ is an invisible organism, rather than a visible organization. It is composed of all the elect of God throughout the ages. Because of their individual union with Christ, Christians have a spiritual unity among themselves, whether or not they are unified organizationally. This unity is therefore spiritual and invisible, not terrestrial and visible. The spirituality and communion of the Body of Christ transcends all limits of culture and time.

S: Security of the Believer

The same grace that saved us preserves us to the end. Using exhortations, warnings and fatherly rebukes, God preserves His elect by His power so that none of them will be lost.

Review Questions

1. The doctrines of grace teach that salvation is solely by _____ without any human contribution.

2. The Reformation doctrines are known today as _____.

3. True _____ or False _____: The doctrines of grace are not controversial today.

4. Sinful human nature wants to be _____ of its own _____.

5. True _____ or False _____: Man is capable of contributing to his own salvation.

6. What does "sovereign" mean?

7. True _____ or False _____: Reality is a consequence of the divine decrees.

8. When did God decree all things? _____

9. Which parts of the individual were affected by sin?

10. The doctrine of the inability of man teaches that a sinner's will is incapable of coming to Christ for _____.

11. True _____ or False _____: Saving faith comes from exercising our own free will.

12. Where does saving faith come from? _____

13. Our inability to contribute to our salvation came about through the fall of _____.

14. True _____ or False _____: The righteousness of the Law is irrelevant to the Christian.

15. God only accepts the _____ of Christ.

16. Can we fulfill the Law for ourselves? Why or why not?
_____

17. Who fulfilled the Law for us? _____

18. When we accept Christ, God grants to us the perfect _____ of Christ.

19. "Justification" means
_____.

20. True _____ or False _____ God chose everyone to be a recipient of His grace.

21. True _____ or False _____ No one can choose Christ under his own power.

22. Before we knew Christ, we were _____ in sin.

23. What accomplished salvation for the elect?

_____

24. The death of Christ not only made salvation a_____, it _____ it.

25. True _____ or False _____ The cross was insufficient to save everyone.

Chapter One

Sovereignty of God

The sovereignty of God is the only legitimate basis for solid faith. When people claim to have faith while denying God's sovereignty, their faith has to be based, to some extent, on human ability. God's sovereignty is crucial to biblical Christianity; without it, "faith" cannot legitimately be called "Christian." Unfortunately, the pervasive influence of humanism in modern society has so affected every domain of our thinking that even conservative Christian pastors neglect preaching God's sovereignty in their pulpits. Such neglect is tragic because the sovereignty of God is the only possible foundation for a stable Christian walk. Any other foundation crumbles under the pressures of life.

This doctrine contends that reality is a product of divine decrees established before the creation of the world. It claims that God controls everything that happens, good or bad. This does not mean, however, that God causes evil or is the author of sin. Nor does He rejoice in the sufferings of His creation. Rather, it affirms that everything is part of a great plan that will inevitably glorify God.

Why is God's sovereignty the only valid foundation for the believer's faith? First, only a sovereign God can guarantee His promises. Only a God who controls everything can be trusted for salvation. If He were not in control of everything, something might prevent Him from saving us. When something as important as our salvation is at stake, can we trust in a God who does not control everything?

Second, if God were not sovereign, we could not derive spiritual lessons from the events of our lives. We would have no way knowing whether God was teaching us something, or if the events of our lives were mere happenstance. Trusting God would be roughly equal to trusting in luck.

Third, the Sovereignty of God is the only basis for giving Him glory. If it is not He who does all the work of salvation, then why should all the glory be His?
And fourth, God's sovereignty is the only basis for prayer. Why pray to a God who is not sovereign? If He does not control everything, He will not be able to answer us.

The very idea of "sovereignty" implies unlimited control and authority. God cannot be "a little bit sovereign" or "mostly" sovereign." Thus, it is illogical to contend, "God is sovereign, but . . ." As soon as we add the word "but," we negate the idea of sovereignty. Such affirmations are like proposing that God is "somewhat infinite," or "almost omnipotent." Any qualification of God's sovereignty is a tacit denial of it. When we study the Covenant in Chapter Eight, we will see why this distinction is so important.

The Foundations of the Doctrine

Four foundational biblical concepts establish the sovereignty of God. In logical order, these are: (1) the divine attributes of omniscience and omnipotence, (2) the immutability **(unchangeableness)** of God's will (3) reality is a product of God's will, and (4) God's ownership of everything.

Foundational Concept #1: The divine attributes of omniscience and omnipotence.

The Bible teaches that God is omniscient, that is, that He knows everything. Acts 15:18 says, "Known to God from eternity are all His works." The Bible also teaches that God **is** omnipotent **or** almighty. Revelation 19:6 says "...because the Lord our God Almighty reigns...."

Denying the Sovereignty of God implies denial of one or both of those attributes. For example, suppose something happens that God did not ordain. That could happen only if

God did not know it was going to happen, or if He lacked the power to prevent it from happening. In the first case, He would not be omniscient. In the second, He would not be omnipotent. If the Bible correctly teaches that God is both omniscient and omnipotent, then it is impossible for anything to happen without His permission.

Foundational Concept #2: The immutability (unchangeableness) of God's will:

The word "immutable" means "never changing." It also carries the idea of "irresistible." (See Hebrews 6:17-19.) Understanding immutability is enhanced by distinguishing between two aspects of God's will: His will of commands, and His will of purposes.

God expressed His will of commands as moral edicts, such as the Ten Commandments. He allows people to sin by transgressing these laws. But when God expresses His will of purposes in His decrees, He allows no one to invalidate or hinder that aspect of His will.

For example, suppose God said, "I command that no one cut down this tree." He would be expressing a divine injunction, an element of His "will of commands." Would God permit someone to cut the tree down? Yes, because God allows people to sin by breaking His commands. Suppose, however, that God said, "My sovereign purpose is that this tree never be cut down." Would God allow someone to cut it down? No. No power on earth, human or demonic, could cut down that tree. God would prevent it.

Were it not for His will of commands, people would

not be allowed to sin. And were it not for His will of purpose, we would lack confidence that God could fulfill His promises.

Since God's will of commands can be disobeyed, God Himself may choose to change His commands. Not only does He allow His commands to be broken, He may even annul them. (The Old Testament ceremonial laws, for example, are no longer binding.) Immutable decrees, on the other hand, never change. And no one can stop God from accomplishing them. This idea is sometimes expressed in Scripture as His "counsels."

> *My counsel shall stand, and I will do all My pleasure.* (Isaiah 46:10)

> *Thus God, determining to show more abundantly to the heirs of promise the immutability of His counsel, confirmed it by an oath.* (Hebrews 6:17)

Other times, the word "purpose" expresses the same thought:

> *...according to the purpose of Him who works all things according to the counsel of His will.* (Ephesians 1:1)

> *For the Lord of Hosts has purposed, and who will annul it? His hand is stretched out, and who will turn it back?* (Isaiah 14:27)

Some texts may not use these terms, but the idea comes across unmistakably.

> *...He does according to His will in the army of heaven and among the inhabitants of the earth. No one can*

restrain His hand or say to Him, 'What have You done?
(Daniel 4:35)

The concept of immutability helps us understand the sovereignty of God by giving us a more secure basis for trusting Him.

Foundational Concept #3: Reality is a product of God's will.
Psalm 33:9 answers the question, "Where does reality come from?": *For He spoke, and it was done; He commanded, and it stood fast.* The Bible teaches that reality derives from divine decrees which were established before the foundation of the world. Hebrews 11:3 says, *By faith we understand that the worlds were framed by the word of God, so that the things which are seen were not made of things which are visible.* This verse can also be translated, "By faith we understand that the epochs of time were established..." The events of history, good or bad, have taken place by the will of God. This includes the most important as well as the most insignificant events.

Revelation 4:11 says, *You are worthy, O Lord, To receive glory and honor and power; For You created all things, And by Your will they exist and were created."* This affirmation is clear. All things owe their existence to God. Occasionally we read in the Gospels, "...this happened that the word might be fulfilled...." This phrase does not mean that a prophet simply predicted the event. It means that the event took place to fulfill the decrees of Scripture. Usually, the people who fulfilled these prophecies were unaware they were doing so – a fact which highlights the basic principle underlying the sovereignty of God: Reality derives from God's will. Prophecy is simply a declaration of that will. Reality coincides with what God has commanded.

Prophecy, therefore, is more than divine foresight. It is a declaration of infallible divine intent. Here are several examples:

1. In Matthew 21:1-4, Jesus told His disciples to look for a certain donkey in a village. Surely the owner was unaware of Zechariah's prophecy concerning Christ's triumphal entry into Jerusalem. The entire incident illustrates the sovereignty of God in the sense that the prophecy was more than divine foresight. It was a divine arrangement.

2. When the crowd came to capture Jesus in Gethsemane (Matthew 26:55-56), He said this occurred to fulfill the Scriptures. The Apostles also consistently affirmed that the arrest and crucifixion took place accordingto a divine plan. Peter, preaching at Pentecost, declared in Acts 2:23: *Him being delivered by the determined purpose and foreknowledge of God,*

3. The Roman soldiers who divided Christ's garments to fulfill "what was written by the prophet" were unaware that they were fulfilling Scripture.

How does God know the future with certainty? Some suppose that God has a mental capacity (like a supreme fortune-teller) that allows Him to peer into the future as if He were looking through a telescope down the corridor of time and seeing coming events. Some teachers even assert that God forms His plans based on this "concept of foreknowledge," and many Christians today believe them. However, to interpret God's foreknowledge strictly in terms of passive divine observation of future events is a defective approach to biblical interpretation.

After all, who created time? Did God create it? Or is time something God discovered by chance in the course of eternity? If God created everything, then He also created time. And if He created time, He also ordained the events that occur in it. If we deny this, we are affirming that God created the universe without purpose, or without full comprehension of what He was creating.

Scripture teaches that God's "foreknowledge" is simply His own understanding of His purposes. His sovereign decrees derive from His purposes, which no power in the universe can change.

Foundational Concept #4: God's ownership of everything.
During a Bible study, a woman asked, "Who owns the earth, God or Satan? With all the wickedness going on, it looks like Satan!" How does Scripture answer her question?

> *...that you may know that the earth is the Lord's.* (Exodus 9:29)

> *...for all the earth is Mine.* (Exodus 19:5)

> *Indeed heaven and the highest heavens belong to the Lord your God, also the earth with all that is in it. (Deuteronomy 10:14)*

> *Everything under heaven is Mine.* (Job 41:11)

> *Yours, O Lord, is the greatness, The power and the glory, The victory and the majesty; For all that is in heaven and in earth is Yours; Yours is the kingdom, O Lord, And You are exalted as head over all.* (1 Chronicles 29:11)

*The heavens are Yours, the earth also is Yours; The world
and all its fullness, You have founded them.* (Psalm
89:11)

Some imagine that when Adam fell into sin, God lost
control of the earth. Note that all the above verses are post-
fall, present tense. With Adam's fall, God lost nothing. The
only loser was Adam.

Let's delve into some specific categories of reality that
God controls:

God is sovereign over:

1. Nature
   *Are not two sparrows sold for a copper coin? And not
   one of them falls to the ground apart from your Father's
   will.* (Matthew 10:29)

According to Jesus, the Father controls the lives of animals. Not even the most insignificant bird can die without
God's permission. The same is true for us, Jesus said. We are
worth much more than the birds, and cannot die until our
Father allows it.

God brought quail to the Israelites. He closed the lions'
mouths in the presence of Daniel. He placed a coin in the
mouth of a fish that Peter would catch. He used frogs, lice
and flies as judgment on Egypt. He sent grasshoppers against
Israel, brought the animals to Noah's ark, and fed Elisha by
means of ravens.

God also manifests His sovereignty through use of the
inanimate. He controlled the Flood and sent darkness, hail
and fire upon the Egyptians. Christ rebuked and calmed the
storm. God caused the sun to stand still at the command of
Joshua.

2. Human Governments and the Human Race

And He has made from one blood every nation of men to dwell on all the face of the earth, and has determined their preappointed times and the boundaries of their dwellings. (Acts 17:26)

The first thing Paul preached to the people of Athens was the sovereignty of God. He knew that this truth is central to a proper understanding of the Gospel. The book of Daniel is a complete study of God's sovereignty in human government. God taught King Nebuchadnezzar a difficult lesson about who establishes kings on the earth. (Daniel 4:17) After having received divine punishment for his pride, the king revealed what he had learned with the words,

All the inhabitants of the earth are reputed as nothing; He does according to His will in the army of heaven And among the inhabitants of the earth. No one can restrain His hand or say to Him, 'What have You done? (Daniel 4:35)

3. The Human Will

Does God overrule the human will? Does God's sovereignty encompass human will and thought? The Scriptures give us the answers.

The king's heart is in the hand of the Lord, Like the rivers of water; He turns it wherever He wishes. (Proverbs 21:1)

For God has put it into their hearts to fulfill His purpose, to be of one mind, and to give their kingdom to the beast, until the words of God are fulfilled. (Revelation 17:17)

If God can easily alter the course of a river, could He not easily change the heart of a king? And if He can change a king's heart, how much more the hearts of ordinary men? God gave Israel favor in the sight of the Egyptian people, and then hardened Pharaoh's heart to show His power.

> *And the Lord had given the people favor in the sight of the Egyptians, so that they granted them what they requested. Thus they plundered the Egyptians.* (Exodus 12:36)

> *Then I will harden Pharaoh's heart, so that he will pursue them...* (Exodus 14:4)

> *There are many plans in a man's heart, Nevertheless the Lord's counsel that will stand.* (Proverbs 19:21)

It is true that human beings do have a will. But human will is not sovereign. Some have erroneously taught and preached that the human will is holy ground on which God Himself cannot tread. However, Scripture is clear that the only inviolable will in the universe belongs to God.

4. Evil

God never compels anyone to sin. Although He is sovereign, He is not the author of sin. People sin because of their sinful natures, not because God compels them to do so. Nevertheless, no one can sin unless God permits them. The Bible reveals that even the circumstances surrounding sinful acts are under God's sovereign control. He has the power to prevent or allow people to sin. It is just as erroneous to declare that God cannot prevent people from sinning as it is to declare that God causes sin.

How does God limit sin and control its circumstances

without being guilty of causing it? Consider this analogy: When a mouse is placed in a cage, it usually runs around the inside walls. Rarely will it just sit in the middle of the cage. Since the mouse's typical natural environment is closed-in areas such as tunnels or underground burrows, it feels more comfortable pressing against something. That is why mice race around the walls of their cages. Their movements are predictable because they coincide with their nature.

The same principle applies to people.

God controls their sinful actions by ordering their circumstances to appeal to their nature. His intimate knowledge of their nature and character allows God to control their sinful actions without being responsible for the sins they commit. God obliges no one to sin, even though He may indeed arrange the circumstances to allow people to express what is already in their heart. The outstanding example of this is the arrest and crucifixion of Christ.

> *Jesus said to them, "Have you never read in the Scriptures: 'The stone which the builders rejected has become the chief cornerstone. This was the Lord's doing, And it is marvelous in our eyes'"?* (Matthew 21:42)

Paradoxically, the rejection of Christ by the Jews was something that Matthew attributed to God. Not only did He know about it ahead of time, but "the Lord has done this." Nevertheless, the Jewish leaders acted according to their own desires, not under compulsion. God's will of command told them not to harm His prophets. But God's will of purpose decreed that they needed to disobey this command in order for redemption to be accomplished.

For truly against Your holy Servant Jesus, whom You anointed, both Herod and Pontius Pilate, with the Gentiles and the people of Israel, were gathered together to do whatever Your hand and Your purpose determined before to be done. (Acts 4:27-28)

The sovereignty of God and human freedom run together through Scripture like train tracks. They complement each another. The Bible writers never considered this a contradiction. They affirmed both, as shown in the preceding text, without the slightest reservation.

Joseph's brothers, motivated by selfishness and hatred, sold him into slavery. Obedience to God was farthest from their minds. Notwithstanding, the Scriptures describe their treachery as a divine act.

So now it was not you who sent me here, but God; and He has made me a father to Pharaoh, and lord of all his house, and a ruler throughout all the land of Egypt. (Genesis 45:8)

But as for you, you meant evil against me; but God meant it for good, in order to bring it about as it is this day, to save many people alive. (Genesis 50:20)

As part of the divine judgment upon David for his sin with Bathsheba and murder of Uriah, God declared that other men "will lie with the wives of David" before all Israel. The way this decree is expressed is very revealing:

Thus says the Lord: "Behold, I will raise up adversity against you from your own house; and I will take your wives before your eyes and give them to your neighbor, and he shall lie with your wives in the sight of this sun.

For you did it secretly, but I will do this thing before all Israel, before the sun." (2 Samuel 12:11-12)

When David's son Absalom temporarily ruled, he committed incest with his father's wives. Oddly enough, this happened as God's judgment on David. God raised up Absalom as a rebel against David and decreed the activities of his rebellion. Nonetheless, Absalom alone was guilty of the sins of rebellion and incest.

How could God decree such things and remain holy? The Lord simply provided Absalom the opportunity to express what was already in his perverse heart. Doctrines of this type are like raw meat for some people . . . hard to swallow. But they are the clear teachings of the Word of God. If God is sovereign over all, then He is sovereign over evil.

Other Scriptural examples of God's sovereignty over evil are:

According to 1 Chronicles 10:4, King Saul killed himself by falling on his own sword. Yet 1 Chronicles 5:14 says that it was God who killed him.

The Apostle Paul teaches that the unbelief of the Jews forms part of the divine plan to include the Gentiles in the covenant of grace. (Romans 11:7-11)

When David fled from Jerusalem, Shimei cursed him. This was wicked on Shimei's part. Nonetheless, David recognized that Shimei did what the Lord had decreed. (2 Samuel 16:11)

Even evil spirits are under God's control. God sent an evil spirit to speak through the false prophets during Ahab's reign. (1 Kings 22:23)

The deceptions that afflict men sometimes come from God as judgments for rejecting the truth. The Sovereign Lord himself chooses the kind of deception suffered. (1 Thessalonians 2:11)

The Scriptures attribute to the Lord the stubbornness of Eli's sons in spurning their father's reproaches. God allowed them to express their wickedness as judgment against Eli for his fatherly negligence and poor example as priest. (1 Samuel 2:25)

Sickness came into the world because of sin. But, "who has made man's mouth? Or who makes the mute, the deaf, the seeing, or the blind? Have not I, the Lord?" (Exodus 4:11)

A hurricane destroys a town. A landslide buries a village. *If there is calamity in a city, will not the Lord have done it?* (Amos 3:6b)

Although Satan is an active agent of evil, divine sovereignty limits his activities. Like a tethered dog, he has freedom up to the length of the leash.

A Comforting Tension

We find ourselves in an uncomfortable philosophical tension between the sovereignty of God and human responsibility that we cannot escape entirely. God considers this tension healthy for us. Our responsibility motivates us to obey Him. His sovereignty gives us a reason to believe our efforts will be successful. God's sovereign power and man's responsibility are twin truths, neither of which can be abandoned. As the late Dr. Francis Shaeffer put it, "For God to be God, and for man to be man, both must be true." [1]

Jesus went to the Cross conscious that "the time of darkness" had arrived. Although He knew that the agents of darkness had captured Him, it was not into the darkness that He commended His spirit. He accepted the cup of suffering from the hand of the Father, not as from Satan. He did not rejoice in the pain, but in the greater good that would result. This is the consolation point in the tension where God wants us to live.

Review Questions

The Sovereignty of God

1. What is the only basis for a solid faith? _____

_____

2. Those who do not believe in the sovereignty of God place their faith in _____ ability.

3. What is the central doctrine of the Bible? _____

_____

4. What happens when one's faith is not based on the sovereignty of God? _____

5. "The sovereignty of God" means that all reality is the result of the _____ _____ established before the creation of the world.

6. Neither good nor _____ escapes the _____ of God.

7. True _____ or False: _____ God is the author of sin.

8. Everything that happens is by the _____ of God.

9. Only a _____ God can guarantee the fulfill-
ment of His promises.

10. True _____ or False _____ Satan can deter God.

11. True _____ or False _____ The events of our lives are chiefly
caused by luck or happenstance.

12. True _____ or False _____ God has decreed all that is to
happen.

13. What is the only basis of giving God glory?

14. We give all the glory to God because He does _____
the work.

15. Is it logical to pray to a God who is not Sovereign?

_____

16. Why is it illogical to pray to a **non**-sovereign God?

_____

17. The word "sovereign" means: _____

18. Today a new "gospel" is being preached that focuses on
_____ instead of the_____ of God.

19. True _____ or False _____ The will of God concerning His
eternal purposes can be resisted or can go unfulfilled.

The Foundations for this Doctrine

1. What are the four biblical foundations for the sovereignty of God?

       a.

       b.

       c.

       d.

2. The Bible teaches that God is "omniscient." This means that He _____.

3. The word "omnipotent" means that God is _____.

4. Give two of God's attributes:

       a.

       b.

5. Which word means "unchangeable?"_____

6. This word can also mean "_____."

7. True _____ or False _____ God allows men to sin.

8. When God has decreed something, He allows no one to _____ it.

9. True _____ or False _____ God cannot go against someone's will.

10. Is God in control of the human will? _____

11. Give a Scripture verse to support your answer to question # 10._____

12. Reality is the product of _____.

13. Human history has unfolded the way it has because of the _____ of God.

14. True or False _____ The important events of history were decreed by God but the insignificant ones happened by chance.

15. Certain prophecies _____ the _____ prophesied.

16. True _____ or False _____ Since God is responsible for everything that happens, He is the author of sin.

Notes:

1. Spoken in this author's presence at L'Abri, Switzerland during a discourse to students, c. 1968.

Chapter Summary — Sovereignty of God

From this chapter we have learned that the Sovereignty of God refers to His absolute control of everything. This is proven by the following facts:

1. His attributes of Omniscience and Omnipotence.
2. The unchangeable and infallible nature of His will of purpose.
3. Scriptural statements that all of reality is a product of His immutable will.
4. God's ownership of everything.
5. His name, Adonai, correctly translated in modern versions as, "Sovereign Lord."
6. His control over nature, nations, the human will and even evil itself.

Chapter Two

Inability of Man

One of lost humanity's favorite myths is the moral neutrality of man's will. Sinners like to imagine themselves in a neutral position, equally situated between good and evil, with the freedom and ability to choose between them.

Sinners usually presuppose the ability to repent and come to God any time they wish. They see themselves in total control of all moral decisions and as the masters of their own destinies. They believe they possess a faculty called "free will," which they define as an ability and right to make impartial choices.

All religious groups affirm a doctrine of free will by some definition. But they differ in the meaning of the word "free." Clearly our wills have limitations, so they are not "free" in every conceivable respect. We cannot will ourselves to sprout wings and fly, nor can we will our intelligence to rise to the level of Einstein's. Our moral struggles teach us that our wills are sometimes our friends and sometimes our determined enemies.

Some groups believe that the free will of man escaped the affects of the fall and remains morally neutral. Others assert that the will was weakened by sin, but that it retains the ability to contribute to salvation. Yet others affirm that sin dominates all human faculties and that sinners are therefore incapable of seeking salvation without an effectual work of grace. Since our view of divine grace ultimately affects our assumptions about the human will, we must carefully define its abilities and limitations.

We affirm the following:

1. That all human faculties are, before the new birth, are dominated by sin and controlled by Satan.

2. That the fallen human will, being dominated by sin, cannot desire salvation nor accept Christ on its own initiative without a miracle of the grace of God.

3. That the new birth is a sovereign act of God, in which the sinner is entirely passive, until the gift of saving faith is granted by God. It is not because we have faith that we are born again. We have faith because we are born again. The human will is not the cause of the new birth.

The word "free" is the source of most of the controversy in this discussion because its meaning is so ambiguous. "Free" can mean "ability," or "permission," or even "neutrality." Therefore we must define our terms before entering into dialogue. Some definitions of "free will" coincide with biblical teaching, whereas others do not.

It is biblically valid to define "free will" in the following senses:

1. The right to choose the good – although the right to do a thing does not prove the ability to do it.

2. The power to choose in morally neutral matters, such as what we will eat for breakfast.

3. The power to choose between external actions of a good or bad nature, such as whether to give to a charity, or deciding to read the Bible instead of a pornographic magazine.

4. The ability to participate in religious practices, such as attending meetings, learning hymns, and praying, even though the person may be unsaved.

But it is unscriptural to teach that unsaved people have "free will" in the sense of:

1. The ability of sinners to repent and accept Christ, entirely on their own initiative.

2. The ability to earn or merit, by deed or thought, the grace of God.

3. A morally neutral mental faculty not controlled by the sinful nature of the person.

4. The faculty of a person's being which ultimately governs his choices.

Importance of the Doctrine

A good grasp of human inability puts our pride in its place. We have no reason to be proud about something we never accomplished. When we see how God overcame the resistance of our obstinate hearts to bring us to Christ, we realize he can preserve us forever despite our sinful flesh. Paradoxically, we experience deep security by abandoning faith in our own moral abilities.

The instant we realize that our will is not the grounds

of our salvation, then the meaning of "grace" becomes clear. We learn that we did not convert ourselves, and that salvation is not a cooperative work between God and man. "Salvation is of the Lord." (Jonah 2:9)

Basis of the Doctrine

Original sin: God created Adam with marvelous gifts. One of these was the ability to choose between good and evil. We call this faculty "free will." When Adam fell into sin, his entire being became enslaved to sin, including his will. The effects of Adam's fall are explained in Romans 5:12-21. In this passage we learn that mankind inherited four things from Adam: sin, death, judgement, and condemnation (Rom. 5:12-21). The guilt of Adam's sin was imputed to his offspring. This biblical truth reveals a central fact of human existence: Man sins because he is a sinner; he is not a sinner because he sins. Man is condemned primarily because of what he *is*; only secondarily because of what he *does*.

The heart, not the will, governs the man: Many presuppose that the will of man decides his actions. This not only contradicts the Scripture, but it also contradicts logic. How can a human will be "free" from the nature of the person in which it is found? One always chooses that which he desires most at the moment. What we desire reflects what is in our heart. So, it is the heart (the internal nature) that dictates a person's choices, not his will. The will is never "free" from the true nature of the creature in which it is found.

Example: Suppose you were starving and were presented with two plates of food. On one plate is a steak and potatoes meal complete with dessert and vegetables. On the other is maggot-infested garbage. Which will you choose? Your desires dictate the choice. On the other hand. if you were a fly, your choice might be different. Our nature determines our desires and our desires determine our choices.[1]

Another example, if you put a duck between a body of water and a sand pile, it will head for the water. Why? Because it chooses according to its nature It's free will is constrained by its nature. This is why Scripture says *"Keep your heart with all diligence, For out of it spring the issues of life" (Proverbs 4:23).*

Christ Himself underlined this principle when He said to the Pharisees:

> *Brood of vipers! How can you, being evil, speak good things? For out of the abundance of the heart the mouth speaks* (Matthew 12:34).

The Bible consistently teaches that the heart of man governs him. (Proverbs 4:23; Matthew 12:33-37; 15:18-19) When a person's heart is dominated by sin, then so is his will.

This principle is well illustrated by the coyote, an animal that cannot be domesticated. By nature it will always be wild, even if raised by humans. Now, let's suppose that during a walk in the woods, we encounter a coyote. We think, "How lovely it would be to have a coyote as a pet! Let's persuade the coyote to come with us!" So we approach the coyote and say, "Coyote, if you come with us, you will have plenty of food. You'll be protected from your enemies. We will be friends, and have a good time." Thinking that we have persuaded the coyote with our proposal, we extend our hand to pick him up. What will the coyote do? Being the kind of animal he is, he will bite.

Here is where we face the central question: Does the coyote have free will or not? This question is a trap. A straightforward and absolute answer does not exist, because it depends on the angle from which we deal with the question. If we define the will of the coyote as the ability to choose between being wild or being domestic, then we would say that he does not have free will. But if we define free will as his ability to choose within the limits of his nature, then yes, he has free will.

This illustration suggests to us a more realistic definition of free will that is more in accord with biblical data. The sinner has free will within the limits of his nature. If sin governs his nature, then he will choose sinful autonomy rather than submission to God since that is what he truly prefers. Before his true preferences will change, God must change his nature. We will see how this happens a little later when we study the New Birth.

<u>Dead? Or Just Sick?:</u> The carnal man may perceive himself as a sinner, but never as morally dead in the sense of total inability to be otherwise. But the Bible says :

> *And you He made alive, <u>who were dead in trespasses and</u> <u>sins,</u> in which you once walked according to the course of this world, according to the prince of the power of the air, the spirit who now works in the sons of disobedience, among whom also we all once conducted ourselves in the lusts of our flesh, fulfilling the desires of the flesh and of the mind, and were by nature children of wrath, just as the others* (Ephesians 2:1-3).

Religious groups that believe in free will (in the sense of moral neutrality), frequently preach as though the sinner were simply sick. They may even use illustrations taken from the field of medicine. The sinner is portrayed as seriously ill but with an ability to accept the "medicine" of the gospel if he wishes. Such a concept is unbiblical. The Bible presents the sinner as dead, not sick. Scripture sees the sinner as totally incapacitated, having no ability to please God if he happens to wish it.

Can the dead raise themselves? "Dead" implies total

inability. But the pride of man will not tolerate such news about himself. Paul continues his discourse in Ephesians 2 by showing that we were conformists (*"...according to the course of this world . . ."*) We went through life under the illusion that all our thoughts were really our own. We thought we were being original, without realizing that we were typical products of a perverse society. The only thing original about us was original sin. Paul reveals that, far from being original, we were puppets of an evil being (*"...the spirit that now works in the children of disobedience..."*).

Finally, Paul shows that our wills were not as free as we thought because they were enslaved by our flesh (*"...fulfilling the desires of the flesh and of the mind..."*). In short, the Apostle Paul appears distinctly unimpressed with the free will of man.

Another text underlining the total inability of man is Romans 3:9-18. According to verse 9, all are *under sin.* This domination is expressed in the following: *"There is none righteous, no, not one; There is none who understands; There is none who seeks after God" (vv. 9-10).*

If none understand, then can sinners grasp the essence of the gospel on their own? Can we allege that sinners have an inherent power of will to seek God if Scripture declares that nobody ever does so? If no one can do good, then may we suppose that sinners possess the power to commit themselves to Christ? If there is no fear of God in them, may we expect them to throw themselves on God's mercy on their own accord?

This state of affairs is illustrated by C.S.Lewis: "Agnostics speak openly about man seeking God. For me, it makes more sense to speak of the rat seeking the cat.... God trapped me." [2]

If there exists the least suspicion that the carnal nature of man could submit to God, Romans 8:7 puts it aside for good: *"Because the carnal mind is enmity against God; for it is not subject to the law of God, nor indeed can be."*

Every Aspect of Man's Being Is Controlled by Sin. The sinner neither understands nor seeks after God (Romans 3:11). His understanding is darkened (Ephesians 4:18). He is blind to spiritual things and considers them foolishness (1 Corinthians 2:14). His mind cannot submit to God (Romans 8:7). He is God's enemy (Colossians 1:21) and blinded by Satan (2 Corinthians 4:4). The thoughts of his heart are evil continually (Genesis 6:5).

His will is controlled by Satan (Ephesians 2:3) so that he is unable to repent without God granting him repentance. (2 Timothy 2:26). He cannot come to Christ unless God draws him (John 6:44, 65).

Someone asked the great theologian Saint Augustine if he believed in free will. He replied, "Of course! Without Christ, we are totally free from all righteousness!"

How Does God Regard the Good Works of the Unsaved?

God does not regard the good works of the unsaved at all, because no unsaved person has ever done a good work.

"Impossible!" exclaimed a doctor in one of my theology courses. "Now I know that you are really off base, professor! I know many fine non-Christians who provide for their families, give to charity, serve the community and are good conscientious citizens. Are you saying that these good works are evil?"

Although the answer may shock the modern humanist culture, the answer to the doctor's question is an uncompromising "Yes!" God counts all the good works of the unsaved, including those that coincide with His commands, as sinful acts. This is true for two reasons: (1) These works proceed from a corrupted source, and (2) They are practiced from impure motives.

The unregenerate heart is dominated by sin, with the self enthroned as the central ruling figure, pursuing its own pride and benefit as the highest value. Until this perverted nature is transformed, and the self dethroned, the entire nature of man is a fountain of corruption. Whatever proceeds from such a fountain will be tainted with corruption, and God's holiness will accept none of it. This is true even if the deed performed is outwardly good. Jesus said, *"Even so, every good tree bears good fruit, but a bad tree bears bad fruit" (Matthew 7:17).*

No wonder Isaiah exclaimed, *"All our righteousnesses are like filthy rags..."*(Isaiah 64:6) If we were to take some filthy rags, make a sweater out of them, and present them to a prince, how pleased would he be with it? That is what the unregenerate do when they imagine that God is pleased with their good works.

Secondly, the motives of the unregenerate are impure. Romans 14:23 says *"for whatever is not from faith is sin."* Whatever is done for any motive other than the glory of God and submission to His will is a subtle form of rebellion.

The unregenerate are never so corrupt as when they are being charitable. The only thing that could be worse is when they are being religious. Such works deceive the unsaved into imagining they are good and that God must be pleased with them. But if the unsaved really wanted to please God, they should do the first thing that God requires: Repent and submit to the lordship of His Son.

"What shall we do, that we may work the works of God?" the multitude asked. In the next verse, Jesus replied, *"This is the work of God, that you believe in Him whom He sent"* (John 6:28-29).

The term *believe* implies something more profound than doing good works. It suggests a personal trust in Christ that leads directly to obedience that dethrones the self. This faith places Jesus in the center of the person's life and gives His will the highest value. No work of any unsaved person, however outwardly good, is an adequate substitute for this self-abandonment.

The unregenerate do good works and religious acts as substitutes for submission. As the Apostle Paul put it, their motive is *"to establish their own righteousness"* rather than submit to *"the righteousness of God"* (Rom. 10:3). The self remains enthroned.

Was this not the problem with the Pharisees? Did not Jesus say that the prostitutes and thieves were closer to the kingdom of God than they? Was this a mere poetic exaggeration? Many works of the Pharisees were in accord with the divine Law since obedience to the Law was the central focus of their movement. In what sense then, were the works of the Pharisees worse than those of prostitutes and robbers? The self-deception involved in a work proceeding from a corrupt heart perverts any deed into a sin worse than those just mentioned. No wonder then that Paul, while discoursing on unregenerate humanity, quoted David saying: *There is none righteous, no, not one (Romans 3:10).*

Is this a brand new doctrine, recently invented? Note that a Christian document written in 1648, The Westminster Confession of Faith, affirms:

> *Works done by unregenerate men, although for the matter of them they may be things which God commands; and of good use both to themselves and others: yet, because they proceed not from an heart purified by faith; nor are done in a right manner, according to the Word; nor to a right end, the glory of God, they are therefore sinful, and cannot please God, or make a man meet to receive grace from God: and yet, their neglect of them*

is more sinful and displeasing unto God. (Chapter 16, Article 7)

God requires good works of everyone, including the unsaved. Yet when the unsaved do them, they sin. If they fail to do them, however, they sin even more. Sadly, their "good works" don't contribute to their salvation, only their condemnation. This is the essence of slavery to sin. Nothing less than the incredible miracle of the new birth can change this hopeless situation.

Selected Questions about Total Inability

Q: How can God make us responsible for doing good if we cannot do it? How can God condemn someone for practicing sin if he can do nothing else?

A: Place a Bible at one end of a table and bottle of wine at the other. Then seat a drunkard between the Bible and the wine and tell him to choose between the two. Which will **he** choose? Obviously he will choose the wine, because that his nature. He has full *liberty* to choose the Bible as well as the *responsibility* to do so. But he lacks the *ability* to choose the Bible. Having the *liberty* does not help him much, because his nature determines what he really wants.

We may misinterpret many Bible texts if we fail to consider this difference between *liberty* and *ability.* Such texts reveal what man *ought* to do, rather than what he *can* do. The sinner is never free from his responsibility to obey God. Yet he is never able to fulfill that responsibility. The Scripture outline below exposes this terrible paradox between the responsibility of man versus his inability.

Responsibility vs. Inability

Come to Christ: Matthew 11:29; Nobody can come: John 6:44.

Repent: Acts 3:19; Repentance is a gift of God: 2 Timothy 2:25.

Circumcise their hearts: Deut.10:16; God circumcises their hearts: Deut.30:6.

Believe: John 3:16; Belief is a gift of God: Philippians 1:29.

Keep the law: Romans 2:13; Nobody can keep the law: Romans 8:4.

Man's inability does not free him from his responsibility to obey God. After all, it is not God's fault that mankind fell into sin. Man's ungodliness does not mitigate God's holy right to require from His creation what is just. The power that compels man to sin is not *external* but *internal*, from within his own nature.

Q: But isn't the will of man sort of neutral, able to choose between good and evil?

A: Many people assume the neutrality of the human will, as though it functions as an organ floating somewhere in our brain, disconnected from our moral state. If this were so, in what sense could we label it our will? How could we be held responsible for what our will decides, if it were independent of what we are?

The Bible always presents the will of man as an extension of the character of the person. In the case of the unregenerate, people always reject Christ until God changes them.

Finally, the Biblical base of our responsibility before God is not our ability, but our knowledge. We see this in Romans 1:18-20. The sinner knows certain things by the revelation of God in nature. But he does not seek God because he prefers sin.

Q: In the first chapter of this book, titled Sovereignty of God, you claim that God controls everything, even the will of man. Doesn't this make man a puppet? Are not the doctrines of the sovereignty of God and the responsibility of man in conflict?

A: There exists a profound philosophical tension between these two aspects of biblical theology. This tension becomes easier to grasp when we remember that God's control is often exercised indirectly through the means of human nature itself. Since a person chooses whatever agrees with his own nature, then God must change that nature to motivate the individual to choose salvation. This way, the will of the person chooses freely, according to the revelation God gives. God maintains his own sovereignty, without forcing the person to act contrary to his will.

The Question of the New Birth: How Do We Come to Accept Christ?

If the sinner has no internal motivation to repent and choose Christ, how then are some converted and others not? We resolve this question by considering the order of events in the new birth. Two different viewpoints exist about what happens in the new birth:

One viewpoint says that the sinner makes a "decision" to believe in Christ which results in the new birth. The sinner produces in himself a degree of faith through an act of his free will. God responds to this act, and rewards him with grace, causing him to be born again. The sinner himself initiates the process. God is the responsive agent, waiting for the human initiative. Faith, according to this view, produces the new birth, so that the sinner contributes to his salvation through faith and obedience.

Another viewpoint says that the sinner is dead in sins, completely unable to believe. God therefore, by a sovereign act, regenerates those whom He has chosen for salvation. The sinner is totally passive in the act of being born again. God is the initiator. Upon being born again, the sinner has a new nature, perceives correctly divine things, and places his faith in Christ. So, being born again produces saving faith, not vice versa. Faith and obedience are *results* of the new birth, not causes of it. The sinner contributes nothing to his salvation. He obtains faith by the righteousness of Christ. (2 Peter 1:1)

Which of these two scenarios is biblical? Examining the Bible texts on the new birth allow us to compare the interplay between "cause" and "effect." Is our obedience the cause of being born again? Or is being born again the cause of our obedience?

CAUSE	EFFECT
John 3:3: *Born again*	*See the Kingdom of God*
Jer.24:7: *God gives a new heart*	*That they may know Him*
Ez. 16:62,63: *God confirms His Covenant*	*And He will forgive their sins*
Ez. 36:26,27: *Gives a new heart*	*Obedience*
James 1:18: *He, of His own will*	*Born again*
Psalm 65:4: *Chosen by God*	*Drawn to Him*

If any doubt remains as to which of the two scenarios mentioned above is correct, then consider John 1:13: *who were born, not of blood, nor of the will of the flesh, nor of the will of man, but of God."*

We can illustrate the point another way by asking the question, "Where does saving faith come from? Does it come from the free will of man, or is it a work of the grace of God?" Another cause and effect outline answers:

CAUSE	EFFECT
Acts 13:48: *As many as had been appointed to eternal life*	*believed*
Acts 18:27: *through grace*	*believed*
Hebrews 12:2: *Jesus, the author and finisher*	*of our faith*
Eph.2:8: *for by grace you have been*	*saved through faith*
Phil. 1:29: *it has been granted*	*to believe in Him*
John 6:65: *granted by my Father*	*come to Me*

Does this mean that the will of man remains an inert faculty before, during, and after salvation? Is our will a mere puppet, manipulated by a celestial puppeteer? No way! When our perceptions change, our other faculties of mind follow. When we *"see the kingdom of God"* (John3:3) through the illumination that regeneration brings, then conversion to Christ becomes inevitable. God reveals Christ to us as so attractive that His very Person becomes irresistible. The irresistible nature of grace consists in this perception, rather than in a forcing of the human will. Christ is just too good to resist when revealed as He is. Such illumination does not transgress any aspect of man's freedom, nor does it do any injustice to those who refuse to look to Christ.

Why God grants this illumination to some and not to others, is a mystery hidden in eternity. The words of the Canons of Dort, a Protestant document written in 1618, express it with beauty and clarity:

> "He opens the closed and softens the hardened heart . . . infuses new qualities into the will, which, though heretofore dead, He quickens; from being evil, disobedient, and refractory, he renders it good, obedient, and pliable; actuates and strengthens it, that like a good tree it may bring forth the fruits of good actions." (Third and Fourth Heads of Doctrine, Article 11)

The correct order of events in salvation is therefore: New Birth, Faith, Justification. Saving faith is a divine gift, not the fruit of human "free will." The new birth is a sovereign act of God. The sinner does not convert himself.

Warning For Pastors

The notion of neutral free will is like a weed in a garden. Just when you think you have it rooted out, it sprouts up again. Of all the erroneous ideas about salvation, this one is the most difficult to eradicate among Christians. As a teacher, you will experience more resistance on this point than any other aspect of the doctrines of grace. Proud human nature persists in its desire to make a contribution to salvation, however minimal.

As we teach the doctrine of total human inability, it is advisable to repeat constantly what we are *not* saying. This helps avoid misunderstandings. For example, it helps to say something like, "We are not saying that man has no will. He does. But sin enslaves his will." Or, "Man is responsible for his actions, although he lacks the strength to fulfill this responsibility because of the power of sin." And, "God commands us to do right because He is holy, not because we can obey properly." And "We are *not* saying that the sinner has no *right* to choose salvation, only that he cannot do so without the grace of God."

As a pastor, it may be costly to clarify to the congregation the doctrine of total inability. But it is worth the trouble to insist on it. God will use your teachings to reveal the true grace of God more clearly to them. You will be giving them a precious jewel that will enrich their lives forever.

The News Of Our Inability Is A Blessing

Many students think they have misunderstood me when they hear me say that understanding our total depravity is one of the finest blessings they can experience. Although they may be used to hearing paradoxes from me, this one surprises them. At least it gets their attention, and prepares them for the following quotation from the great reformer Martin Luther:

> "On The Comfort Of Knowing That Salvation Does Not Depend On Free Will:
> I frankly confess that, for myself, even if it could be, I should not want 'freewill' to be given me, nor anything to be left in my own hands to enable me to endeavor after salvation; not merely because in face of so many dangers, and adversities, and assaults of devils, I could not stand my ground and hold fast my 'freewill' (for one devil is stronger than all men, and on these terms no man could be saved); but because, even were there no dangers, adversities, or devils, I

should still be forced to labor with no guarantee of success, and to beat my fists at the air.

If I lived and worked to all eternity, my conscience would never reach comfortable certainty as to how much it must do to satisfy God. Whatever work I had done, there would still be a nagging doubt as to whether it pleased God, or whether He required something more. The experience of all who seek righteousness by works proves that; and I learned it well enough myself over a period of many years, to my own great hurt. But now that God has taken my salvation out of the control of my own will, and put it under the control of His, and promised to save me, not according to my working or running, but according to His own grace and mercy, I have the comfortable certainty that He is faithful and will not lie to me, and that He is also great and powerful, so that no devils or opposition can break Him or pluck me from Him. 'No one, ' He says, 'shall pluck them out of my hand, because my Father which gave them me is greater than all' (John 10:28-29). Thus it is that, if not all, yet some, indeed many, are saved; whereas, by the power of 'freewill' none at all could be saved, but every one of us would perish.

Furthermore, I have the comfortable certainty that I please God, not by reason of the merit of my works, but by reason of His merciful favor promised to me; so that, if I work too little, or badly, He does not impute it to me, but with fatherly compassion pardons me and makes me better. This the glorying of all the saints in their God." [3]

Questions on Total Human Inability

Certain verses appear to support the idea of free will, in the sense of moral neutrality. We can organize these according to the following categories:

<u>Verses showing that man chooses evil</u>: Some suppose that because man can choose to sin, he must also have the ability to choose righteousness. This would be like saying that a log has the ability to float upstream merely because it can float downstream. Insisting that man has the power to choose evil

is no evidence that he can choose submission to God without a work a grace.

<u>Exhortations and commands to choose the right:</u> Occasionally people quote verses in which God commands us to choose the good. God commanded Israel to keep His Law. Is this evidence that man can keep the Law? Of course not. The New Testament shows us that nobody keeps the Law. The Law was given, rather, to reveal what man cannot do, rather than what he can do. Why then take verses out of the Law to prove moral free will?

God commands us, "be perfect." Does this prove we have an innate ability to be perfect without God's grace? Certainly not. Otherwise we would not need Christ at all. Why then imagine that unconverted mankind has the ability to choose good on the mere basis of a command? God commands people to do right because He could hardly command them to do otherwise. Being good Himself, He could not command them to do evil. God commands us to do right because He is just, not because we are capable.

<u>Verses which show that man is responsible for his actions:</u> We do not deny that people are responsible for their conduct. We only deny that responsibility implies ability. The only kind of verses which could refute the doctrine of total human inability would be those showing that sinful people, without God and without grace, can convert themselves. Such verses do not exist. Commands, exhortations, examples of sinners choosing evil, and explanations regarding our responsibility, have nothing to do with the question.

Review Questions

1. A popular myth among humanity is

_____.

2. This myth is the basis of every distortion of the

_____.

3. True or False: _____ All faculties of the sinner are dominated by sin, except his will.

4. True or False: _____ The human will, on its own, can never desire salvation apart from a work of grace.

5. True or False: _____ The new birth is a sovereign act of God in which the sinner is entirely passive, until his nature has been renewed, enabling him to respond correctly.

6. The myth that we have been refuting in this chapter is called _____.

7. The correct definition of grace becomes clear when we realize man's _____.

8. True or False: _____ Salvation is a co-operative work between God and man.

9. What are a couple of the benefits that a Christian obtains through understanding the doctrine of Total Human Inability?_____

_____

10. What happened to Adam's will when he fell into sin?

_____

11. The guilt of Adam's sin is attributed to

_____.

12. Which of the following sentences is the most correct according to our understanding of the fall of Adam?
    A. We sin because we are sinners.
    B. We are sinners because we sin.

13. Which of the following faculties of human nature determine what people will decide?
    A. The Will
    B. The nature/heart
    C. His parentage

14. Which of the following sentences is correct?
    A. The heart governs the will.
    B. The will governs the heart.

15. True or False: _____ The sinner is spiritually sick, but not spiritually dead.

16. Those who reject the doctrine of Total Human Inability are confused with regard to the difference between the _____ to choose, and the _____.

17. The phrase "freedom to choose" means:
    A. The sinner has the power to choose the good.
    B. Elements within the sinner's own nature oblige him to choose evil.
    C. God obliges him to choose evil.

18. Explain in your own words why the verses in the categories below are not valid evidences to show that the will of man is "free to choose salvation, apart from the intervention of grace.

A. Verses showing that man chooses sin.

B. Exhortations and commands to choose the good.

C. Verses showing that man is responsible for his actions.

19. The biblical basis for human responsibility is _____.

Notes:

1. This illustration is a revised version taken from a sermon on Predestination by Tim Keller, Pastor of Redeemer Presbyterian Church in New York, 2001.
2. Quoted from C.S. Lewis, in *Gathered Golden*, John Blanchard, Evangelical Press 1989 pp. 74.
3. Martin Luther, *The Bondage of The Will*   Section XVIII , No.783

Chapter Summary — Inability of Man

From this chapter on the Inability of Man, we learned that man is unable to contribute anything, neither by his works or his will, that could attract the saving grace of God. This is proven by:

1. Mankind inherited Adam's sin, along with its consequences: death, judgment and condemnation.
2. Mankind has lost all ability to will or do anything to contribute to his salvation.
3. The heart, not the will, governs a person's choices.
4.   Fallen man is spiritually dead, not merely sick.
5. Every aspect of man's being is controlled by sin, including his will.
6. No unregenerate person has ever done a work that is acceptable to God, nor ever could.
7. Man is responsible for obeying God, whether he has the ability to do soor not. No necessary connection exists between responsibility and ability.
8. Regeneration precedes saving faith. We believe because we are born again, not vice versa. The correct order of events in salvation is regeneration, faith, justification.

Chapter Three

Justification By Faith

The war-cry of the Reformation, "Justification By Faith!", resounded throughout Europe during the 16th Century. Thousands lost their lives rather than renounce this doctrine. War broke out in various countries over it. Why such controversy? Because this doctrine upset the concept of personal salvation that had been accepted for centuries.

Toward the end of the 16th Century, something in the Bible astonished a German priest named Martin Luther. It was Paul's declaration in Romans 1:17 that struck him. ("the just shall live by faith") God illuminated his heart, and Luther understood that merit had nothing to do with salvation. Armed with this revelation, he continued his studies in Romans and came to understand the centrality of justification by faith to biblical teaching. This incident contributed to a rediscovery of the theology of the Bible and launched the movement known as the Reformation.

Importance Of The Doctrine

Why is this doctrine essential? First of all, it frees us from confusion about the basis of our acceptance with God. The moment we realize that God roots our acceptance in the righteousness of Christ alone, rather than our own degree of perfection, we experience a profound relief from unwarranted fear. Second, it helps us avoid legalism by focusing on righteousness as an inwardly accomplished fact rather than external practice. Performance-based righteousness *always* leads to legalism. And third, it helps us in prayer. The moment we realize that the answers come because God accepts us in Christ, rather than because of how good we've been lately, we are free to approach God with greater boldness.

Definition Of The Doctrine

Justification is a legal declaration by God that a person is righteous with respect to the divine Law because of the perfect righteousness of Christ, imputed by faith in Christ. A doctor once said that the best way to understand good health is to study diseases. In much the same way, a good way to grasp the essence of justification is to understand what it is *not*.

Justification does *not* refer to the process of spiritual growth in the life of the Christian. ("Sanctification" is the correct term for that.) Justification deals with the issue of our *legal* relationship with the Father as compared with His holy Law. A common mistake among Christians in the study of justification is to imagine that justification means "to be made righteous." Actually, it means, "to be *declared* righteous," or "to be *vindicated*."[1]

Nor is justification a reward for our faith. As we saw in the previous section on the new birth, saving faith is a work of divine grace. Although God requires faith as a condition of justification, we must not assume that justification is a *reward* for our faith. Let us not assume that a *consequence* is the same as *reward*.

Neither must we suppose that faith replaces the requirements of God's moral law. This Law (represented by the Ten Commandments) forms part of an eternal covenant and is irreplaceable. Some accused the Reformers of teaching that if we have faith, we need not perform any good works. The reality of the matter is that the works of sinners are not valid for salvation because they proceed from a corrupted source.

So, the *works* are not accepted if the *person* is not accepted. The person is accepted only on the basis of the imputed righteousness of Christ, granted through faith alone. The central idea in justification is how the perfect righteousness of the Law accrues to our account despite our inability to keep the Law. According to the Bible, Christ alone accomplishes this as our substitute under the Law. Let's use the following questions to clarify the definition above.

1. Does God require that the righteousness of the Law be fulfilled in the Christian?

Yes. Romans 8:4 says *"that the righteous requirement of the law might be fulfilled in us who do not walk according to the flesh but according to the Spirit."* God requires that the righteousness of the moral law be fulfilled in us. Here is where some believers get confused. They read verses that affirm that we are not under the Law and that we cannot be justified by it. From this they draw the illogical conclusion that the Law no longer has value and that God does not require in them the righteousness that it represents.

The Jews fully understood that the Law represented the righteousness of God. So they supposed that justification came by obedience to the Law. They erred in failing to grasp that no one can keep it consistently. Paul showed us that the righteousness that the Law represents comes to us by means of faith in Jesus Christ, as a gift from God. Both we and the Jews agree on one essential point: God always requires the righteousness of the Law. We differ from the Jews in how we *obtain* that righteousness. They believe that keeping the Law is the means. We believe that God grants it as a gift, through faith in Christ alone.

Thus, it is essential to understand that the law was

never annulled as a righteous requirement. It remains in effect in another sense. The Law has a *defining* function. It defines important moralistic terms, such as "righteousness" and "sin." First John 3:4, for example, asserts that "*sin is the transgression of the Law.*" Logically, the word "sin" would be meaningless without the Law.

Similarly, Paul says in Romans 5:13, "*For until the law sin was in the world, but sin is not imputed when there is no law.*" And he says in Romans 3:20, "*Therefore by the deeds of the law no flesh will be justified in His sight, for by the law is the knowledge of sin.*" The Law is the only standard of righteousness that the Bible recognizes. Without the Law, there would be no sin, and therefore condemnation would be impossible.

The problem we have with the divine demands of the Law is that fallen humanity cannot keep them. As Paul says in Romans 8:7: "*Because the carnal mind is enmity against God; for it is not subject to the law of God, nor indeed can be.*"

2. How does the righteousness of the law become credited to us?

Here we touch on a beautiful principle in biblical theology: The Substitution of Christ. Jesus was our substitute under the Law. Christ fulfilled the Law in our place in two senses. First, He lived a perfect life under the Law, fulfilling all its demands (Romans 3:21-26). Second, Christ accepted in His body the punishment that the Law requires for transgressors: death.

> For what the law was powerless to do in that it was weakened by the sinful nature, God did by sending his own Son in the likeness of sinful man to be a sin offering. And so he condemned sin in sinful man, in order that the righteous requirements of the law might be fully met in us, who do not live according to the sinful nature but according to the Spirit. (Romans 8:3-4)

Paul develops this theme in Galatians 4:4-5: *"But when the fullness of the time had come, God sent forth His Son, born of a woman, born under the law, to redeem those who were under the law, that we might receive the adoption as sons."* This clarifies why Paul believed it was unnecessary to invalidate the Law as a condition of salvation. *"Do we then make void the law through faith? Certainly not! On the contrary, we establish the law"* *(Romans 3:21).* The death of Christ was necessary precisely because the moral law is eternal and is always in effect. If it were not so, no one would be counted a "sinner" and Christ need not have died.

Grace does not consist in a change of the conditions for salvation from something that man cannot do (keep the Law), to something he can do, (believe in Jesus). Both the righteousness of the Law and the faith to receive it come from Christ by Grace alone.

3. Is faith the basis of our justification?

This is, in a sense, a trick question because the answer is technically *No.* Faith is not the basis of our justification. The perfect righteousness of Christ is the basis. Faith is simply the necessary means by which that righteousness is received.

To illustrate, let's consider the process of laying the foundation for a building. The framework of the foundation represents us. The cement we pour into the framework represents the perfect righteousness of Christ. The metal conduit through which the cement is poured represents faith. Before the cement arrives, the framework is empty. No foundation exists. The same with us. Without Christ, we are empty of all righteousness. We have nothing to contribute and everything to receive. God Himself installs the conduit of faith. Through this conduit, God pours the "cement" – the perfect righteousness of Christ – and creates the solid foundation on which we construct our lives.

Sanctification is like building the house once the foundation has been laid. It is a process that continues throughout life. The degree of success varies between believers. (Some trust Christ more than others in building their houses.) But justification is not a process. It is a divine act accomplished at the moment of the believer's conversion to Christ. It can never be repeated. Why? Because the perfect righteousness of Christ can never change. Sanctification, on the other hand, means "to be *made* righteous" or "to *be* righteous" or "set apart" (for holy use).[2] It involves the daily practice and outworking of righteousness in our life.

As we mull this over, it becomes clearer why some believers feel insecurity concerning their acceptance with God. They confuse sanctification and justification. They imagine that their eternal acceptance with God depends on their degree of sanctification. The result is emotional and spiritual instability because sanctification is a process that can vary. Since their sanctification seems to fluctuate, they assume their acceptance does too.

Basing our acceptance with God on our degree of sanctification is a formula for disaster. We move immediately into performance-based righteousness, rather than faith-based righteousness. Since our performance is imperfect, we open wide the door to doubts, insecurities, and a lack of boldness before God and man.

Legalism finds fertile ground in those who base their acceptance with God on their degree of sanctification. To assure themselves of God's approval, they invent rules and regulations by which to measure their performance. (Dress codes; don't go to movies or dances, etc. It is interesting to notice that the rules they invent are always less stringent than the demands of God's moral laws. They need rules and regulations because faith is an abstract concept, and difficult to use as an objective measurement of performance. Spiritual failure and emotional instability are the inevitable products of legalism. This happens because the so-called faith of legalistic believers is only faith in their fleshly ability to be obedient. This is faith in self, not faith in Christ.

Consistent with the teachings of Paul, Dr. Charles Hodges discusses the substitution of Christ with these words,

> *Hence Adam is the type of Christ. As the one is the head and representative of his race, so the other is the head and representative of his people. As the sin of the one is the ground of the condemnation of his pos-terity, so the righteousness of the other is the ground of the justification of all those who are in him.* [3]

Since justification is an absolute, then the great Apostle Paul is no more justified than a new babe in Christ. More sanctified, yes, but not more justified.

A minister friend started a Bible study with these words: "There is no one on earth more righteous than I!" A lady in the audience exclaimed, "How can you say such a proud thing?" He explained, "I did not say, 'I am more righteous that anyone else.' I only said that there is no one else who is *more* righteous. I have the perfect righteousness of Christ imputed to me as a free gift. But this is true of every other believer in the world, including you!"

Ironically, the weakest believer can say the same. He cannot, of course, claim the same understanding, maturity, rewards in heaven or degree of sanctification. But his acceptance with God is equivalent. In heaven, we will be no more justified than we are now. The glory we will experience may vary between believers. But it will be placed on the most glorious and immovable foundation that could exist – the righteousness of Christ Himself.

The entire fourth chapter of Romans illustrates how the perfect righteousness of Christ becomes ours. Paul uses Abraham as the example. Abraham lived more than four hundred years before the Law of Moses. He had no written Law of God. The only thing he had was his conscience and his faith. So Paul comments, *"Abraham believed God, and it was accounted to him for righteousness" (Romans 4:3)*. However, his faith was not *in place of* righteousness. Faith was the *means* by which God accomplished his justification. The word "for" in Greek here, is a difficult word to translate. Its meaning is something like, "with a view to." It does not mean "instead of."

4. For whom is justification by faith designed?

Romans 8:30 says, *"Moreover whom He predestined, these He also called; whom He called, these He also justified; and whom He justified, these He also glorified."* Justification by faith is reserved for the elect. The eventual glorification of the elect is as certain as any other part of the chain of events that Paul mentions in this text.

5. Can a believer lose his or her justification?

Only if Christ can lose His righteousness. Romans 8:33 says, *"Who shall bring a charge against God's elect? It is God who justifies."* God accepts no accusations of sin against His elect and sanctified people with regard to their eternal destiny. Why not? Because Christ has granted them His righteousness. And the perfect righteousness of Christ never changes.

This makes no sense to the carnal mind because sin is always supposed to result in condemnation. But God has driven a wedge called "justification" between sin and condemnation. In jurisprudence, a trial cannot take place until the court receives a written accusation. If for some reason the judge does not acknowledge the accusation, then no trial can take place and the prisoner goes free. In refusing to acknowl-edge the accusation, the judge is under no obligation to say to the prisoner, "Oh, what a wonderful person you are!" In fact, he need not even make a declaration of "not guilty." In refus-ing to acknowledge the accusation, the judge declares only that the accusation is legally unpresentable.

Imagine this scene in heaven. Satan appears and says, "God, look at what your kid did! She gossiped. She has a loose tongue. She caused all sorts of problems in the church!" God replies, "Who do you think you are coming in here and accusing my kids! You are not even a part of the family. I can take care of my own family and do not need your advice to do it. Get out!" Satan leaves.

End of story? Not quite. After God slams the door on Satan, He says, "Daughter, come here a moment. There is a little matter I'd like to discuss with you." Right there is the difference between justification and sanctification. And the difference is hardly theological hairsplitting. It is the differ-ence between defeat and victory, legalism and freedom, in our relationship to the Father. We are free to assume that the Father is delighted with us until He says otherwise. He is proud of His kids and rejoices over us. He is truly glad to have us in the family. Zephaniah 3:17 says, *"He will take great delight in you . . . he will rejoice over you with singing."*

Does this mean that God's kids have a license to sin? No, it does not. Romans 6:1-2 says, *"What shall we say then? Shall we continue in sin that grace may abound? Certainly not! How shall we who died to sin live any longer in it?"* Paul sees justi-fication as a license to pursue righteousness with a new confi-dence, looking ahead to His infallible victory. He declares that freedom from sin, and the sincere pursuit of righteous prac-tices, characterizes those justified by faith in Christ alone.

Review Questions

1. True or False: _____God requires that the righteousness of the Law be fulfilled in us.

2. True or False: _____Faith is the basis of our Justification.

3. True or False: _____God accepts faith in Christ as a substitute for righteousness.

4. True or False: _____The word justification means "be made righteous."

5. True or False: _____Justification is something that God accomplishes in us when we accept Christ and can never change.

6. True or False: _____Justification is a process.

7. True or False: _____Sanctification is a process.

8. True or False: _____Sanctification is merely a theoretical doctrine and has no practical applications in the life of the believer.

9. True or False: _____Now that we are justified by faith, the Law ceases to have any value.

10. True or False: _____God's intention was that all of humanity should be justified.

11. The war-cry of the Reformation was: _____

12. The Catholic priest of the 16th Century who discovered in

the Bible the doctrine Justification by Faith was named:

13. The doctrine of Justification by Faith serves to:

    a.

    b.

    c.

14. Christ was our substitute under the Law in two senses:
    In His _____
    and in His _____.

15. True or False: _____It is possible for a believer to lose his or her justification.

16. True or False: _____God does not accept accusations against His chosen and justified people.

17. What is the chief characteristic of those who are justified?

Notes:

1. This is the meaning of the corresponding Greek verb, DIKAIAO. A couple of good examples showing the 'vindication' aspect of its meaning are: Rom.3:4- "That You may be justified in Your words . . . " The text refers to the 'justification', (i.e., 'vindication'), of God relative to human accusation. It could hardly be said that 'justified' here means 'MAKE righteous. Another example is 1Ti.3:16, in which Paul, referring to the incarnation of God in Christ, says, " God was manifested in the flesh, Justified in the Spirit." That is, the work of the Spirit through Christ vindicated His claims. Jesus, being God, was not MADE righteous, but rather declared by the Spirit to be so, and thus vindicated with regard to all accusations.

2. The 'process' aspect of sanctification occurs in such texts as Heb. 10:14, "For by one offering He has perfected forever those who are being sanctified." Notice the interesting parallel between the accomplished fact of redemption, (has perfected forever), versus the continuous present tense application via sanctification as a process, (being sanctified).

3. Hodges, Charles: *Systematic Theology,* Vol.2, pp.203

Chapter Summary — Justification by Faith

From this chapter on Justification we learned that:

1. Justification means 'declared righteous,' not 'made' righteous.
2. God requires the righteousness of the Law to be fulfilled in us.
3. Justification is a declaration from God that a person is entirely righteous relative to His holy Law.
4. Christ was our substitute under the Law and gained a perfect righteousness for us.
5. None of the works of unregenerate people can be counted as good because their works are based on their own autonomy rather than submission to God.
6. Righteousness is a free gift of grace given through faith in Christ.
7. Justification can never change because the righteousness of Christ can never change.

Chapter Four

Election By Grace

A story: "In a far away city there lived a man of rare qualities. He was a famous sculptor and practiced martial arts also. In both domains he was a superb master. Unfortunately, several of his friends misunderstood him. Some believed that his occupation as a sculptor revealed effeminate traits, delicate and sensitive. Others assumed that a karate master would be hard and violent, and they feared him.

So, he invited his friends to a private party. Before his friends arrived, the man took a mass of clay and divided it in two parts. He molded one part into a beautiful sculpture, a country scene with people, animals and flowers in a lovely forest. He painted the work and hardened it in a furnace. With the other part, he formed a simple square block and also hardened it in the furnace. When the friends arrived on the appointed day, he took out the first sculpture, the beautiful forest scene, and set it before them.

"What a delightful work of art!" they exclaimed. "How delicate and charming! You are such a sensitive artist!"

The master replied, "Thank you for your compliments. But I practice another art as well."

The guests glanced at one another, puzzled by this statement. They watched as the master stepped into his adjoining studio and carried back to the room a big square chunk of hardened clay.

"Certain arts do not require the same kind of sensitivity as sculpturing," he said in a deep voice. The master put the block down on the table in the middle of the room and took a short step back from it. He raised his right hand high over his head and with a powerful cry slammed it down on the block. The hardened clay smashed into pieces, dust flying.

The guests understood. True, the master was gentle and delicate – but also strong and dangerous. It was wise to stay on his good side."

The Lord God is like this artist. Some see him as a loving Father who would never harm anyone. Others perceive him as a mighty God who establishes justice, punishes and reproves. Both are correct. The Apostle Paul put it like this: *"Therefore consider the goodness and severity of God: on those who fell, severity; but toward you, goodness, if you continue in His goodness. Otherwise you also will be cut off"* (Romans 11:22).

In the story above, the sculpture represents the elect people of God and the block represents those who are reprobate. Neither the grace of God nor His righteous judgment could be manifested if He had not allowed Adam and Eve to fall into sin. Only sinners can be either graciously redeemed or righteously judged. God's mercy and His divine justice are complimentary and interdependent. This truth leads us to both love God and fear Him.

The Controversy Over Election

If some day you are struck with the mischievous desire to provoke an argument among Christians, simply drop the word "predestination" into a conversation! For some, this word is a treasure-house of comfort that helps them understand God. For others, it is the worst of slanders on the righteous character of God. A lack of biblical support for the concept is not the reason for this controversy.

Predestination is four times easier to prove from Scripture than *is* the deity of Christ. In the New Testament we have around ten verses that directly express Christ's deity. But more than forty address the doctrine of predestination. Yet the same Christians who readily defend the deity of Christ fight furiously against the idea of predestination.

Later we'll see why this occurs, but first, let's define some terms.

The Meaning Of Predestination

Predestination means "destined beforehand." It refers to the divine arrangement of circumstances to accomplish God's decrees which He established from before the foundation of the world. Election refers to the divine decree to call out from among lost humanity certain individuals to be beneficiaries of the free gift of salvation. God did this without reference to merits, the state of the will, or foreseen faith in the elect. Yet He did not act arbitrarily.

God obliges no one to sin. Neither is He the author of anyone's sin. He simply allows the non-elect to continue in the direction of condemnation they themselves have chosen. In theology, we call this "reprobation."

Although the concepts of Predestination and Election are similar, they are not exactly the same. Predestination is the more general term and refers to God's arrangement of reality to accomplish His decrees. Election focuses on the decree to save certain persons in particular. For example, suppose we want to teach a horse to run in circles. First, we choose a horse. This corresponds to election. Then we construct a circular corral so that he will be obliged to run circles rather than some other pattern. This corresponds to predestination. The corral represents the circumstances of life within which we have liberty of action. So, we have liberty in one sense but not in another. God arranges the circumstances of our lives to accomplish His eternal decrees for us.

Just How Important Is The Doctrine Of Election?

Election is like a spotlight that shines on the word "grace." Without this light, grace could be perceived as a reward for human works. This would be a drastic misunderstanding that could effect our entire walk with God. Since the correct definition of grace is "unmerited favor," grace is, by definition, independent of any human contribution. The moment we grasp this concept, it becomes clear that grace and election are inseparable. We must hold to both, or neither. Paul expressed this bond with the words,

> *Even so then, at this present time there is a remnant according to the election of grace* (Romans 11:5).

The Biblical Evidence

Only two arguments exist to refute the doctrine of election: The concept of justice, and the concept of foreknowledge.[1] Paradoxically, these also constitute the two most powerful arguments in *favor* of election. Because they backfire on their proponents, we call them The Paradox Proofs. Let's see how this works.

<u>Argument From The Concept Of Justice:</u> Anti-predestinarians say, "Predestination cannot be true because God would be unjust to chose some and not others. If the will of God is irresistible, how could God hold man responsible for sin?"

Paul anticipated this objection in Romans 9:14-16:

> *What shall we say then? Is there unrighteousness with God? Certainly not! For He says to Moses, 'I will have mercy on whomever I will have mercy, and I will have compassion on whomever I will have compassion. So then it is not of him who wills, nor of him who runs, but*

of God who shows mercy.'

Anti-predestinarians seem to forget that Paul antic-ipated their objection and dealt with it firmly. Moreover, he does so without the slightest apology. In fact, he shows little inclination to even answer the objection thoroughly. He simply re-affirms God's right to show mercy, or withhold it, according to His good pleasure. He emphasizes that election does not depend on the human will any more than it does on human works. *"So then it is not of him who wills, nor of him who runs ..."* (v. 16).

This seems hardly designed to satisfy anti-predestinar-ians. But to make matters worse, he rebukes them for their presumption in asking the question!

> *You will say to me then, 'Why does He still find fault? For who has resisted His will?' But indeed, O man, who are you to reply against God? Will the thing formed say to him who formed it, 'Why have you made me like this?'"* (Romans 9:19-20).

Paul answered this objection before it ever came out of the mouth of the first anti predestinarian. The paradox in this 'proof' is right there. If absolute sovereign election were not what Paul were teaching, he would not have anticipated the primary objection to it, nor bothered to rebuke the objectors.

To assert that election is unjust is to talk back to God. Paul seems reluctant to enter into the philosophical details, not because they are unanswerable, but because he under-stands too well the impossibility of satisfying the pride of men who consider themselves captains of their own fate and masters of their own soul. Since pride, rather than intellec-tual acumen, is the real basis of the objection, then a rebuke is more appropriate than an explanation.

Nevertheless, God is indeed rational and just. So Paul exposes a hidden fallacy behind the objection: We all merit condemnation. If God were to leave the whole human race in condemnation, He would be doing no injustice to anyone. How then could God be guilty of injustice for saving any-body? Some of us receive mercy. Others receive justice. Nobody receives injustice. Quite right that it does not seem fair. It is *more* than fair!

The concept of *fairness* is rooted in the idea of merits or equal treatment. If Johnny gets a piece of cake, then I should get one also. That is only *fair*. If Joe gets a good attendance award at school and if my attendance is equal to his, then I deserve one also. If the other guy gets something good, then I *deserve* the same thing under the same terms. Likewise, if God gives salvation to my neighbor, then certainly I *deserve* the same thing if I am no worse than he is.

These analogies depend upon the assumption of human dignity. Relative to mundane matters like a piece of cake or an attendance award, human dignity may have some value. Relative to the holy Law of God, it has no value at all because both my neighbor and I deserve to be thrown forth-with into hell.

Our only appropriate response to the question of election is to shut our mouths and tremble. God reserves for Him-self the right to do with His creation as He pleases.

<u>Argument From The Concept Of Foreknowledge:</u> Does God choose some and not others because He sees beforehand their faith and obedience? Those who answer 'yes' to that question base their view on two verses. These are:

> *Elect according to the foreknowledge of God the Father, in sanctification of the Spirit, for obedience and sprin-kling of the blood of Jesus Christ: Grace to you and*

peace be multiplied (1 Peter 1:2).

*For whom He foreknew, He also predestined to be con-
formed to the image of His Son, that He might be the
firstborn among many brethren* (Romans 8:29).

Although at first glance it might appear that these texts
defend the foreknowledge argument, they actually do the
opposite. Here's why:

1. It is not saving faith that God could have foreseen
because, saving faith itself is based on predestination. Acts
13:48 says, *"And as many as had been appointed to eternal life
believed."*[2] If faith itself is produced by grace, then God is the
cause of it. Therefore faith is not something passively foreseen
by God. *"... those who had believed through grace" (Acts 18:27).*
On this point Augustine commented, "Man is not converted
because he desired it, but because it was ordained to be so by
election." [3]

2. Neither was it good works that God foresaw. Ephesians 2:10 says that the works of God's people are just as predestined as those who performed them. No positive quality
exists in man for God to foresee. *"For we are His workmanship,
created in Christ Jesus for good works, which God prepared beforehand that we should walk in them" (Ephesians 2:10).*

In fact, the Greek word translated *foreknowledge* also
means *foreordained.* In the verses quoted above, obedience
is a *result* of foreknowledge and not the *cause* of it. Peter
declares, *"...unto obedience,"* not *"because of obedience."* Paul
also expresses in Romans 8:29 *"to be conformed,"* not *"because
he saw that they were."* Ironically, these two verses support
predestination rather refute it.

It is interesting that in 1 Peter 1:20, the apostle uses this
same word, foreknowledge, in connection with the coming
of Jesus, and is translated "foreordained." It would be ridicu-

lous to say that the Father simply 'foreknew' that Jesus was going to come. The same with Acts 2:23, *"Him, being delivered by the determined purpose and foreknowledge of God, you have taken by lawless hands, have crucified, and put to death."*

When used in relationship to divine activity, the term foreknowledge clearly means foreordained. Rather than refuting the doctrine of predestination, this term supports it. Thus, it is a "paradox proof." Further, no causal link exists in the Bible between election and any divine foreknowledge about how people are going to react to Him. For example, Jesus said, *"Woe to you, Chorazin! Woe to you, Bethsaida! For if the mighty works which were done in you had been done in Tyre and Sidon, they would have repented long ago in sackcloth and ashes"* *(Matthew 11:21)* If these populations would have repented at seeing miracles, why didn't God send them a prophet? The answer: They were not a chosen people.

God chose Israel as His people *despite* His foreknowledge of their rebellion.

> *But to Israel he says: 'All day long I have stretched out My hands To a disobedient and contrary people* (Romans 10:21).

> *Even so then, at this present time there is a remnant according to the election of grace* (Romans 11:5).

When God sent Ezekiel to the Jews, He warned them that they would reject the message. Why did God bother? Because the Jews as a nation were God's chosen people according to God's sovereign will, not because He foresaw that they would respond favorably. But even more peculiar is God's declaration if He had sent Ezekiel to a heathen nation, they would have listened! Why then didn't God do that? Only the doctrine of election explains it.

> *For you are not sent to a people of unfamiliar speech*
> *and of hard language, but to the house of Israel, not*
> *to many people of unfamiliar speech and of hard lan-*
> *guage, whose words you cannot understand. Surely,*
> *had I sent you to them, they would have listened to you*
> (Ezekiel 3:5-6).

In I Corinthians 2:7-10, Paul assures us that God has predestined for us a special wisdom, hidden from the rulers of this world. God knew that if this wisdom had been revealed to the rulers of this world, they would not have crucified His Son. Why then did not God reveal it to them? Because this wisdom is for us, not them.

> *But we speak the wisdom of God in a mystery, the*
> *hidden wisdom which God ordained before the ages for*
> *our glory,which none of the rulers of this age knew; for*
> *had they known, they would not have crucified the Lord*
> *of glory. But as it is written: 'Eye has not seen, nor ear*
> *heard, Nor have entered into the heart of man The things*
> *which God has prepared for those who love Him.' But*
> *God has revealed them to us through His Spirit. For the*
> *Spirit searches all things, yes, the deep things of God* (1
> Corinthians 2:7-10).

It would be perfectly reasonable for God to base His elective decrees on some positive reaction in man, *if* man were capable of seeking God. But Romans 10:20 denies that fallen man has any such ability. *"I was found by those who did not seek Me; I was made manifest to those who did not ask for Me."* What are we then to think of people who appear to be seeking God? It could be that God is indeed drawing them. This then is a grace of God. Or they may be seeking a god of their own imagination that will accept them on the basis of their own imagined goodness. But in any case, fallen man, without grace, cannot seek for God.

Common sense also excludes divine foreknowledge as an explanation of election. For example, suppose God foreknew that Mr. John Doe would be born in circumstances that would provoke him to reject Christ. God, being omnipotent, could change those circumstances to predispose him to accept Christ. The inference is inescapable. If God does not change those influences, then it is because Mr. Doe is not elect. Interestingly, both Scripture and reason reveal that the concept of divine foreknowledge supports, rather than refutes, the doctrine of sovereign election.

Mystery, Mystery, Where Is The Mystery?
Three Illustrations From Romans Nine

Every theological system eventually crashes headlong into inscrutable mystery. This occurs because God has infinite intelligence whereas we don't. It is only natural to expect Him to say or do things that puzzle us. Paul's long discourse in Romans 9-11 is a good example: It ends with:

> *Oh, the depth of the riches both of the wisdom and knowledge of God! How unsearchable are His judgments and His ways past finding out!* (Romans 11:33)

Every system of theology encounters points it has difficulty explaining. We call these, 'points of mystery.'

For those advocating a "foreknowledge" view of election, the point of mystery resides in the question, "Why did God bother to create those whom He knew would be lost?" The foreknowledge view seems to answer the fairness question but fails to address the idea of immutable sovereign decrees.

The predestinarian may feel smug at this point until someone asks, "Why did God chose some and not others?" Predestinarians easily answer the sovereignty questions, but often stumble over the fairness issue. So if neither side can solve its particular mystery question, how do we decide which system is valid? Shall we assume neither is able to do so with certainty and just pick the one we like best? This would be an easy out if no means existed to decide the issues. However, a means does exist. We can answer the mystery questions with certainty.

The solution lies in taking a look at where the Bible places the point of mystery. Romans 9 defines which of the two views is correct by identifying the point of mystery. Let's look at how the text does this.

Paul expresses his arguments via three striking illustrations: Jacob and Esau, Pharaoh, and the Potter and The Clay.

1. <u>Jacob and Esau (vv. 6-13):</u> Paul teaches two parallel concepts: national election, and individual election. Paul is not speaking only of national election. From verses 6 to 8, and in verse 24, the focus of his teaching is on individual election. "

> *For they are not all Israel who are of Israel, nor are they all children because they are the seed of Abraham; but, 'In Isaac your seed shall be called.' That is, those who are the children of the flesh, these are not the children of God; but the children of the promise are counted as the seed"* (Romans 9:7-8).

He underlines the same point in verse 27 by making a distinction between saved Jews and lost ones. *"Though the number of the children of Israel be as the sand of the sea, the remnant will be saved."*

In verse 11, Paul focuses on Jacob and Esau to illustrate election: *"for the children not yet being born, nor having done any good or evil, that the purpose of God according to election might stand, not of works but of Him who calls."* Jacob and Esau were twins. Yet before they were born, God chose Jacob instead of Esau, without regard to the characteristics foreseen in them.

If God had chosen Jacob because He foresaw in him a heart sensitive to the things of God, the verse would read something like, "...that the purpose of God may remain according to a good heart and not according to Him who calls." Paul does everything in his linguistic power to make it clear that election **is** grounded in God's effectual call, not in any foreseen quality in Jacob. That explains why Paul takes the trouble to point out the elective decree was already in place before they were born, without regard to any evil or good they would do.

In verse 13 Paul links divine love with election: *"As it is written, 'Jacob I have loved, but Esau I have hated.'"* God loves by His free elective choice, not because the elect are lovable. His love is a powerful and personal force that drives Him to seek, save, and preserve His elect. He is the Shepherd who seeks the lost sheep. His love is active, not passive; personal, not general; voluntary, not forced.

Jacob and Esau symbolize the elect and the reprobate. Where, then, does the love of God fit in? Three basic viewpoints deal with this delicate and complex subject. We'll take a look at all three, and leave it to the reader's discretion to decide which carries the most weight.

In theology, we often discover that various views of an issue may be supported by evidence. One of these is the issue of God's love. We ask, Who does God love and how much? Does God love everyone equally? Does he love Adolf Hitler in hell as much as the Apostle John in heaven? Did he love Pharaoh as much as Moses? Is the love of God both universal and equivalent? People answer these questions in different ways.

A very common view today among Christians is that the love of God is both universal and equivalent. He loves everyone, and He loves everyone to an equal degree.[4] He loves no one more that anyone else. Two snags can tangle this view. The above text, Romans 9:13, is the toughest snag. Even if we accept that the love of God is universal, it seems clear that it cannot be equivalent. It seems impossible to make the phrase, *"Jacob I have loved and Esau I have hated"* mean that God loved Esau in the same way as He loved Jacob. Even if we grant that *"hated"* means an inferior kind of love (as some have suggested) a distinction of some sort remains. Worse still, the prophet Malachi indicated that the divine hatred toward Esau resulted in the total annihilation of his descendants. Total annihilation seems a rather peculiar way to express affection.

A second snag in the "universal" view is less obvious, but once noticed, is equally striking. Every reference in the Bible to the love of God is associated with His people. A concordance verifies this. Some texts even make a point of linking the love of God to the elect. *"Therefore, as the elect of God, holy and beloved,…"* (Colossians 3:12); *"knowing, beloved brethren, your election by God"* (1 Thessalonians 1:4). Even the well-known John 3:16 is connected to believers, and therefore does not support the universal view. Even if the word "world" meant "everybody who ever lived," nothing indicates that the love of God is of the same sort for everyone.[5]

A lady approached the venerable Baptist preacher Charles Spurgeon and mentioned that she was bothered by the phrase, *"… but Esau have I hated."* Spurgeon answered, "That point is not what bothers me, madam. What bothers me is that God was able to love Jacob!"

We *must* preach the love of God in a balanced way, by affirming with it the holiness God and the Lordship of Christ. Otherwise, such a proclamation may produce in the mind of the hearer the concept of God as a benign heavenly grandfather who would never harm anyone, whose love is passive and frustrated, who loves everyone in general without loving anyone in particular, who amounts to an impotent, frustrated deity who hopes in vain that man will respond to His pleadings to love Him. Such a concept of God is popular in our day because He represents no danger at all. Should we then be surprised why we live in a generation that has lost its fear of God?

Throughout the New Testament, the Apostles preached repentance toward God and faith in the Lord Jesus Christ, but seemed to reserve the message of love primarily for believers. A few texts on this point are Psalm 5:5, Proverbs 15:9, John 13:1, John 14:21-23, Romans 1:7, Romans 11:28, 2 Thessalonians 2:13, Hebrews 12:5-6, and James 2:5.

A second viewpoint on God's love affirms that He loves all humanity in His capacity as Creator, but loves His children in His role as Father. His love as Creator extends to all because His children are also part of His creation. But His love as Father does not extend to all because not all are His children. This view is based largely on blessings that God distributes to everyone indiscriminately. These include preservation of the race (1Timothy 4:10), rain and harvests (Matthew 5:45), and provision of habitation for the various people groups (Acts 17:26).[6] This view declares the universality of God's love, but distinguishes between the elect and the reprobate. The diagram 1 expresses this.

The third view divides the elect and reprobate into separate categories: God loves His elect, and hates the reprobate. It assumes that the illustration of Jacob and Esau must

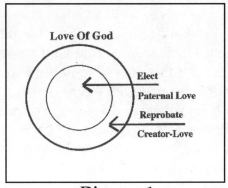

Diagram 1

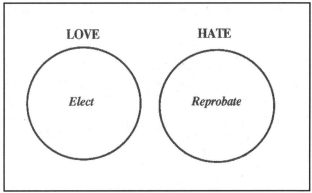

Diagram 2

be taken literally. The diagram 2 illustrates this.

Let's focus now on the principle point in Romans 9 which Paul expresses as: *"So then it is not of him who wills, nor of him who runs, but of God who shows mercy" (v. 16).*

Paul introduces a devastating conclusion with the words, *"So that."* This verse excludes both will and works as a basis in man for election. Yet Paul never denies the existence or value of the human will. He simply denies its relevance to the question of election. To Paul, it would be like disputing the quality of a cement foundation for a house, when the house will never be built there anyway.

2.Pharaoh (vv. 17-18): Paul now introduces the difficult doctrine of reprobation which teaches that God passes some by
in His elective decree. If God elects some for salvation, then
obviously, those not chosen are not elect.

Election and reprobation do not work the same way.
The "rules" are different. In election, God changes the sinful
heart to dispose a sinner to accept Christ. In reprobation, God
changes nothing at all. He simply leaves sinners in the state
they themselves have chosen and prefer. God does not need
to act to make sinners reprobates. He simply leaves them
alone. They sin quite efficiently without any outside help at
all!

Several texts in Exodus indicate that God hardened
Pharaoh's heart. Others say that Pharaoh hardened his own
heart. Both statements are right. God hardens the heart of
reprobates by confronting them with truth. Pharaoh reacted
in accord with his own sinful nature and hardened his own
heart.

God does no injustice to reprobates. He allows them to
have what they want most – their own sins. Their most profound desire is for God to leave them alone and not interrupt
their autonomy or their pleasures. This illustrates one of history's greatest paradoxes: Some receive from God what they
least desire (until God changes their sinful hearts) and will
be grateful forever. Others receive what they most desire and
will regret it forever. This is no injustice. It is truly a poetic justice. Let's remember that we all deserve Pharaoh's fate. Before
Christ found us, we all had the same hard heart. The only difference between Pharaoh and us was God's mercy, not any
moral superiority in His elect. *"Therefore He has mercy on whom
He wills, and whom He wills He hardens" (Romans 9:18).*

3. The Potter and the Clay (vv. 19-22): Some have argued that Paul's potter and clay illustration could scarcely refer to an individual human being. People, they say, have a will; whereas, vessels of clay do not. However, Paul does not deny that man has a will. He simply rejects the notion that the will of man is the basis of election. God, the potter, "prepares" vessels for dishonor (the reprobate) as a demonstration of the righteous judgment of God, and He prepares vessels of honor (the elect) to express the glory of His grace.

The contrast is clear: The love and mercy of God toward the elect are eternal; so is His holy anger toward the reprobate. These two groups are at the extremes of eternity and can never be reconciled. Everyone is one vessel or the other; no one falls in between.

Again, human pride is dashed to the ground, and God's truth triumphs: We exist for God's glory and not He for ours.

Ephesians One: The Question of Causes and Effects
(Read verses 3-11)

All our spiritual blessings have their cause in the elective decree of God before the foundation of the world. Thus, election is the cause and the spiritual blessings are the effect of His decree. One of these blessings is holiness: *"that we should be holy and without blame before Him in love"* (v. 4). Paul does not leave us the luxury of reversing this order, nor does he imagine that foreseen holiness is the cause of our election. Otherwise, we would have to say that God put us in Christ because He foresaw that we would be holy, not because he saw that we were sinners and needed it. This would be "another gospel" of merits, rather than of grace alone.

According to this passage the spiritual blessings derived from election are:, holiness (v. 4); love of God (v. 5);

adoption (v. 5); complete acceptance (v. 6); redemption by the blood (v. 7); wisdom and spiritual intelligence (v. 8); knowledge of the will of God (v. 9); inheritance in heaven, (v. 11); and sealing by the Holy Spirit (v. 13).

Several arguments have been proposed to attempt to refute this literal interpretation of Paul's teachings. A common one asserts that the election mentioned in Ephesians simply refers to the divine plan to include Gentiles in the offer of salvation, not the election of specific individuals. The problem with this interpretation is that Paul was not a Gentile, yet included himself in the context. He was a Jew, and used the terms "we" and "us" in such phrases as *"we have obtained an inheritance."* He included himself in the plan of predestination. Then in verse 13 he says, *"in whom you also."* This clearly shows that his thinking was not limited to Gentiles specifically before verse 13. In verses 1-12, he must have been referring to Christians in general, not to Gentiles specifically.

The Precedence of Election

Our salvation is like a multi-faceted diamond ring. The base of the ring is election, and supports the diamond. The base must be prepared beforehand before the jewel can be mounted. Likewise, it is essential that the decree of election precede every aspect of our salvation. Let's look at some of the other facets of salvation, outside of Ephesians 1 that demonstrate the precedence of election.

Acts 13:48 tells us that election precedes saving faith: *"And as many as had been appointed to eternal life believed."* Ephesians 2:10 says that election precedes good works: *"For we are His workmanship, created in Christ Jesus for good works, which God prepared beforehand that we should walk in them."* Election also precedes the covenant: *"I have made a covenant with My chosen" (Psalm 89:3);* and effectual call: *"Moreover whom He predestined, these He also called" (Romans 8:30).*

Knowledge of our election is a source of inexhaustible joy. Its profound, practical benefits incite us to "the praise of the glory of His grace" and produce stability like no other teaching can (Ephesians 1:6; 2 Peter 1:10).

How Do We Know We Are Elect?

Paul opened his letter to the Thessalonians by saying, *"remembering without ceasing your work of faith, labor of love, and patience of hope in our Lord Jesus Christ in the sight of our God and Father, knowing, beloved brethren, your election by God" (1 Thessalonians 1:3-4)*. He knew that these brothers were elect because he recognized in them the three cardinal virtues: faith, hope and love. He understood that the development of these qualities characterize the elect.

Though God wants us to have the assurance of our election, but this confidence may not come easily. Diligence in the practice of these virtues is central to assurance. It shouldn't be based on the fact that we have simply prayed a sinner's prayer or made a so-called "decision" for Christ. Those are not biblical proofs of election. The Bible focuses on character instead. For example, Peter exhorts us, *"Therefore, brethren, be even more diligent to make your call and election sure, for if you do these things you will never stumble" (2 Peter 1:10)*.

Some unbelievers may, by force of human will, develop these virtues to a certain degree. However, human efforts eventually fail, and the fallen nature will come blasting through. The process of perfection is long-term, and only possible through the power of the Holy Spirit. Persistence in this process is the key characteristic of the elect.

Summary

The doctrine of predestination exposes a key question in redemption: "What is man's contribution to his salvation?" Human nature supposes that salvation must be a cooperative work between God and man. God responds to man's efforts by granting grace. If this is correct, then grace is not sovereign. The various false gospels differ as to precisely what it is that man contributes to his salvation. Some want to contribute good works and penitence. Others respond that the only thing we contribute is faith through our good will, along with the resolve to be obedient to evangelical norms.

Self-deception is at work in such gospels because both miss the central point: The issue is not *what* we contribute, but whether we contribute anything at all! Predestination confronts us with our own corrupt nature like no other teaching can. It exposes our total inability and leads us to a glaring confrontation with God's holy and sovereign nature. It assaults human self-sufficiency mercilessly. It exposes humanism of every brand, both secular and religious. Human pride cannot stand up to an assault like this. Human pride, even among the regenerate, *must* oppose the doctrine of predestination, because it cannot bear the demeaning thought that man contributes nothing at all to his own salvation. Pride must choose to be dashed to pieces, or to turn away.

This doctrine is as painful as it is glorious; brutal as it is comforting; bitter as it is sweet. It gives strength in trials, perseverance in persecution, confidence in prayer and security in our relationship with the Father. It puts man in his place. But more importantly, it puts God in *His* place as sovereign.

For the believer, predestination soon becomes more than a doctrine. It draws us into a magnitude of experience where we touch something hidden and profound. We feel eternity in our souls.

Questions About Election

Question No. 1: In 2 Peter 3:9 we read, "...*not willing that any should perish but that all should come to repentance.*" Does this text contradict the concept of election?

Answer: The context of the verse confirms election, rather than contradicts it. In verse 8, Peter refers to his readers as "beloved," and Colossians 3:12 tells us that the beloved of God are the elect. More importantly, the *promise* Peter refers to in verse 9 is not the promise of the offer of salvation for all humanity, but rather the promise to the Church of Christ about its final liberation.[7] We know this because verse 10 speaks of the promise of the second coming of Christ and the Day of the Lord. Peter exhorts Christians troubled about the delay in Christ's return by reminding them that the delay is for a purpose. When every member of the body of Christ has been added, Christ will return.

Another aspect of the above question is this: If God intended to save all, then why not send Christ immediately? Is God unaware that 5 million children are born in the world every day, and that according to statistics, only a small fraction of these will come to salvation? Therefore, considering both context and logic, the only possible interpretations to the phrase *"...not willing that any should perish"* resides in the Divine intention to redeem all the elect, and not humanity in general.

Let's run through 2 Peter 3:9 again with some comments to clarify it:

The Lord is not slack concerning His promise [of the second coming of Christ] *as some count slackness, but is longsuffering toward us*[the elect], *not willing that any* [of the elect] *should perish but that all* [the elect] *should come to repentance.*

Question No. 2: Paul affirms in 1 Timothy 2:4 that God *"desires all men to be saved and to come to the knowledge of the truth."* Does this suggest that God wants everyone to be saved and that therefore Election and Reprobation are false?

Answer: The context of the phrase "all men" brings to light the correct interpretation. In verse 1, Paul exhorts Timothy to pray for "all men"; then in verse 2, he adds that he refers to kings and all those in authority. Paul exhorts Timothy not to limit his prayers to the poor only, but to extend his vision to the ruling classes also. We see, in this way, that the phrase "all men" means "all without distinction of classes," not "all without exception of person." The expression "all men" is repeated hundreds of times in the Scriptures. In fewer than ten percent of the cases does it mean "all of humanity." Normally it means "all sorts of people."

Another text that helps us to understand this concept is Titus 2:11. Paul says: *"For the grace of God that brings salvation has appeared to all men."* At the time this was written, the message of Christ had not been revealed to the Chinese or the Aztecs. Paul emphasizes here the universality of the Gospel, which transcends all racial and cultural barriers.

Finally, in 1 Timothy 2:7 Paul reveals his thoughts on "all men" by saying, " *I was appointed a preacher and an apostle...a teacher of the Gentiles in faith and truth."* In Paul's thinking "all men" means Gentiles also and not just Jews only.

Question No. 3: If Election is true, why bother to evangelize?

Answer: We evangelize because God commanded it. Although God is all powerful, and can use any means He chooses, He has ordained the preaching of His Word as the means to save His Elect.

Question No. 4: If election is true, why pray to God to save souls?

Answer: Likewise, if salvation depends on the will of man, why bother to pray to God? Why not erect an altar dedicated to "The Will of Man" and pray to it? For if God is waiting passively and impotently in heaven for man to decide, then we are wasting our time to pray to Him.

As with the preaching of His Word, so God uses prayer as a means to accomplish His purposes. He gives us the privilege of participating in those purposes.

Other Evidence

Although the Bible is the story of God's elective decrees, the limitations of this study prevent a detailed analysis of all the texts on election. We recommend that the student avoid a common error in the study of this theme: Getting lost in the details and forgetting the overall pattern of the Bible. The pattern is simple: God, by His sovereign will, chose a people for salvation, without taking into account their merits. God instituted a Covenant of Grace for them, provided a blood sacrifice to confirm and guaranteed the preservation of the participants. The order of events is clear: Election, Covenant, Sacrifice, Preservation. Any other order **is** clearly unbiblical and therefore mistaken.

Other texts on election are: Mark 13:20; John 13:18; Romans 11:5; 1 Corinthians 1:27-28; 1 Thessalonians 1:4; 2 Thessalonians 2:13; 2 Timothy 1:9; Titus 1:1.

Review Questions

1. Election is controversial because: (Mark One)
    a. Not much evidence exists in the Bible to support it.
    b. Human pride rebels against it.
    c. This doctrine dishonors God.

2. Predestination means:

3. Election means:

4. True or False: _____ The words predestination and election are similar but not exactly the same.

5. True or False: _____ Those who deny the doctrine of election do not correctly understand the meaning of the word "grace."

6. The two "paradox proofs" are:

    a.

    b.

7. In what text does Paul anticipate the objection based on the concept of justice? _____

8. The only correct doctrine concerning election is that it tempts man to say, "_____"

9. Paul answered the objection based on the concept of justice by: (Mark one)

    a. An apologetic attitude in the fact of the objection.

    b. Answering the objection by a detailed explanation.

c. Affirming the right of God to do with what belongs to Him, without explanations or apology to anyone.

10. To suggest that God is unjust in His decrees of election is no less than _____.

11. In election, some receive _____, others receive _____, but no one receives _____.

12. The word "foreknowledge" means _____.

13. There are three things that do not qualify as causes of election, because they also are works of grace in man. These are:

   a.

   b.

   c.

14. When the Scriptures use the word "foreknowledge" in reference to God's activities, it can only mean _____.

15. True or False: _____ In the Scriptures, there exists a clear relationship between election and the way in which God foresees that people will respond.

16. To support the idea of "foreknowledge" as refutation of the doctrine of election, it is necessary to deny one of two important attributes of God. These are:

a.

b.

Questions on Romans 9:

17. Romans 9 contains three illustrations of Election. These are:

    a.

    b.

    c.

18. True or False: _____ In the first illustration, Paul speaks only of personal election.

19. Some say that in Romans Nine, Paul is speaking of national election only and not about personal election. Some refutations of this are:

    a.

    b.

20. Jacob and Esau are symbols, respectively, of the _____and of the _____.

21. True or False: _____ God chose Jacob rather than Esau because He saw beforehand that Jacob had a good heart.

22. True or False: _____ God has a special, love for the elect that He does not have for humanity in general.

23. The love of God is _____ and not
    _____.

24. The most important verse in Romans 9 to show that election has no basis in the will of man is
    _____.

25. In the second illustration, that of Pharaoh, the doctrine of
    _____ is revealed.

26. Explain in your own words why election and reprobation do not work exactly in the same way.

27. True or False: _____ In the third illustration, Paul denies categorically that man has a will.

28. The reprobate exist to demonstrate _____.
    The elect exist to demonstrate _____.

29. True or False: _____ God's primary concern is the welfare of mankind.

Questions on Ephesians One

30. All spiritual blessings belong to us because: (Mark One)

    a. God chose us before the foundation of the world.

b. God foresaw us beforehand as being in Christ.
c. We are evangelicals.

31. Some of the spiritual benefits belonging to the Elect are:

32. Two of the anti-predestinarian arguments, in the face of Ephesians One are:

    a.

    b.

33. True or False: _____ The phrase "chosen in Christ" means "chosen because we were in Christ."

Questions On Reprobation

34. True or False: _____ The doctrine of reprobation is agreeable to man.

35. To cause a person to be reprobate, God must: (Mark One)

    a. Oblige the person to sin, whether the person wants to sin or not.
    b. Tempt the sinner.
    c. Act in accord with the sinful choices that the sinner himself desires to make.

36. True or False: _____ God does no injustice to the reprobate in condemning them.

37. True or False: _____ God is completely passive in repro-
    bation.

38. God hardens the hearts of the reprobate by: (Mark One)

    a. Hiding from them the truth of the gospel.
    b. Presenting them the truth, letting them act in accord
       with their own sinful natures.
    c. Simply ignoring them.

39. True or False: _____ God gives the gift of faith to all.

40. True or False: _____ God always works for the salvation
    of everyone.

Notes:

1. All other arguments are really just variations of these.
2. The 'Translator's Handbook', a guide used by Wycliffe translators
   tells us that, "Those who had been chosen for eternal life is a phrase
   which occurs frequently in rabbinic literature. The meaning is clearly
   that those whom God had chosen became believers, and the translator
   must not attempt to weaken this meaning.
    Chosen for eternal life may thus be rendered as "whom God had
   selected in order that they would have eternal life." *A Translator'S
   Handbook On The Acts Of The Apostles* By Barclay M. Newman AndEu-
   gene A. Nida, Copyright 1972.
3. Quoted in *Gathered Gold*, John Blanchaard , Evangelical Press 1989, pp
   74.
4. It was not so common four hundred years ago during the Reformation. Some theologians feel that the popularity of this view among
   modern Christians owes itself more to the pervasive influence of
   Renaissance Humanism than to Reformation Theism.
5. The term 'world', as used throughout the Bible, and especially by
   John,has at least five meanings. Of the 105 times that John uses it,
   perhaps we may interpret 11 this way, but even those are disputable.
   Normally the intent of the word is to communicate that the Gospel is
   for all ethnic groups, and not just for Jews exclusively. John, like the
   other Apostles, seemed particularly concerned about communicating

the universality of the Gospel message. This was a key controversy in his day.

6.   In theology we call these blessings, 'Common Grace', as distinguished from personal salvation, which is 'Special Grace'.
7.   We agree that the Gospel is an offer to all, but this is not the point of Peter's discourse here.

Chapter Summary — Election by Grace

From this chapter on Election, we learned that:

1.   Election is God's decree from all eternity, to save certain people from among lost humanity.
2.   Predestination means the divine arrangement of circumstances to guarantee the accomplishment of His decrees.
3.   Election has nothing to do with foreseen faith, good will or works in the elect.
4.   Saving faith is a gift of grace given to the elect.
5.   The two arguments against election are actually the main proofs for it. These we call 'Paradox proofs', because they prove the opposite of what they intended. These paradox proofs are Argument from Foreknowledge and Argument from Justice.
6.   God has a special love for His elect people that He has for none else.
7.   When God passed by the non-elect in His decree of election, he did no injustice to them because He owes them nothing.
8.   We know we are elect by observation of God's grace in our lives.

Chapter Five

Sacrifice of Christ

In the previous chapter we saw that God divides humanity into two camps: the elect and the reprobate. We saw that the reprobate demonstrate the righteous judgment of God. The question we must now consider is whether God sent Jesus to save reprobates.

The answer is obvious. God is too wise to send Christ to save those whom He did not elect.

Before proceeding we must clarify a misunderstanding: The sufficiency of the cross for all mankind has never been questioned among Christians. The sacrifice of Christ contains enough virtue and power to save a whole universe of sinners. It could even save the devil and all his demons – if that had been the intention of the Father. Whether or not an individual is savable depends on the *intentions* of the Father, not on His *ability*. The Cross is unlimited in saving power.

Yet clearly a limitation of *some* sort exists at *some* point, since not all are saved. Defining our terms will help clarify where the point of limitation is located.

Definition of the Doctrine

The death of Jesus guarantees the salvation of all the elect. He fulfilled all the conditions of salvation so that man contributes nothing to his salvation. Even the necessary conditions of salvation such as faith, obedience, repentance, and perseverance were provided for in that moment of death. The faith and obedience of the elect are born out of the cross, not out of the free will of man. God owes no thanks to the elect for their obedience. Quite the reverse. They owe it all to the cross.

When we preach about the completed work of Christ, we mean that the cross accomplished the purposes for which it occurred, no more and no less. It was not a partially failed enterprise. In theology, we use the term "efficacious" to describe this concept. If we say that a hammer is efficacious, we mean that it can drive nails into a board. If we say that a detective is efficacious, we mean that he is good at catching crooks. Logically, we cannot say that a thing is efficacious if it fails to fulfill its purpose. Essentially, if any of those for whom Christ died could perish, then we cannot call the Cross "efficacious."

Other terms used to describe this doctrine are "Particular Redemption" and "Limited Atonement," which we will use interchangeably. The terms express that the Father sent Jesus with the precise mission of saving certain individuals, not with the intention of saving humanity in general. The opposite of this teaching is called "Universal Atonement."

We will deal with two inseparable questions in this section: (1) What effect did Christ's sacrifice have on those for whom He died?", and (2) "For whom did Christ die?" Answering the first question also answers the second.

If the faith and the obedience of the elect are ultimately attributable to their own human will, rather than the efficacy of the cross, then Christ is a partial Savior and deserves only partial glory. We would have a performance based relationship with God, rather than one grounded in a work completed by God Himself. Every false religion in the world, and every distorted version of the Christian gospel says, "Do!"

The true one says, "Done!"

The Biblical Evidence

<u>Particular Redemption In The Gospel of John:</u> Before the Reformation, those who taught that Christ came to save the elect were sometimes called "Johannian scholars," because they based much of their thinking on the Gospel of John. The term "Augustinian" was also used because St. Augustine in the fifth century was one of the first theologians to teach the doctrines of grace systematically. These scholars taught that the correct doctrine regarding redemption could be deduced from the following considerations:

(1) Christ came to accomplish the will of the Father, (6:38)

(2) The will of the Father was to save only those He gave to Christ, (6:39)

(3) Christ accomplished with complete success the work the Father had given Him   to do, (17:4).

The logical conclusion is that Christ came to save the elect, not the entire world, and that He accomplished this task with complete success. He did not come to save the whole world and then return to heaven having succeeded only in part.

Of Sheep and Goats: John Chapter 10

In the tenth chapter of John, Jesus revealed that He came to give His life for *"the sheep . . . I lay down My life for the sheep" (v. 15).* A dear brother rose up in church to give a testimony. He explained how the Lord had changed him from a goat to a sheep. His intentions were very good, but the illustration was defective. Goats never change into sheep, nor sheep into goats. A lot can happen to sheep. They can get lost or dirty, be stolen, injured, or killed. But they can never change into goats.

John 10 illustrates both the limitation and the efficacy of Christ's sacrifice. Christ knew the sheep as His own before He came to save them. I am the good shepherd; and I know My sheep, and am known by my own. (v.14) They were His, but they were dead. *"I have come that they may have life, and that they may have it more abundantly" (v.10)*. They needed resurrecting. Christ exchanged His life for the sheep via His sacrifice for them. *"The good shepherd gives His life for the sheep" (v. 11)*. Notice He did not say, "I came to give my life for sheep and goats."

Nevertheless, the sheep are obliged to *believe*, right? Naturally! But faith is not the reason they are sheep. They receive the gift of saving faith because they are sheep. Faith is a result rather than a cause of salvation. Notice verse 26: *"...But you do not believe, because you are not of My sheep."* Jesus does not teach here that we are sheep because we believed. He says we believe because we are sheep. J.I. Packer underlines this by saying,

> "The Cross's saving power does not depend on
> faith being added to it; its saving power is such
> that faith flows from it." [1]

Verse 28 says that the sheep receive eternal life. They do not become sheep by the act of receiving eternal life because they were already sheep.

What determines that some become sheep and others not? Their own faith or free will? No. They are sheep because of an elective decree of the Father. The work done in them is because they were given to Jesus, who never fails.

Those the Father Gave to Him

Jesus repeats throughout the Gospel of John the phrase, "those whom the Father has given to me." This phrase speaks to the Father's saving intentions. Let's open our Bibles and analyze the following verses:

1. *John 6:37-45, 65*:

First, we belonged to God the Father by a divine decree before we belonged to Christ. *"All that the Father gives Me will come to Me"* (v. 37). The phrase, *"those whom the Father has given to me" is* the key to understanding the entire Gospel of John. God gave certain people to Christ as gifts, in order to save them. He did not send the Savior to save whom He could, but to save those the Father gave Him.

Second, those the Father gave Him will come to Him. How do they come? The Father will draw them, (v. 44.) Coming to Christ **is** not something generated out of their own initiative because they are incapable of doing so. The Father plants the idea in them and through the revelation of Christ, makes them willing to come (v. 44).

Third, the will of the Father is the determining factor in everything. Christ knows that the Father will accomplish His purposes. In verse 39 Christ refers to the Father's will. *"This is the will of the Father who sent Me, that of all He has given Me I should lose nothing, but should raise it up at the last day."* It is impossible that any of those whom the Father gave to Christ should perish because God's irresistible will undertakes to accomplish salvation through an infallible Savior. In similar terms, Packer exclaims,

> "Christ did not win a hypothetical salvation for hypothetical believers, a mere possibility of salvation for any who might possibly believe, but a real salvation for His own chosen people." [2]

A good summary of this entire concept is found in verse 44. It merits special attention because it contains, in one form or another, all the doctrines of grace we have studied up to this point: *"No one can come to Me unless the Father who sent Me draws him; and I will raise him up at the last day.* In one brilliant statement, Jesus declares the following teachings:

(1) Total Inability: Unsaved people are totally incapable of choosing Christ by their own initiative
(2) Effectual Call: The power of the Father alone brings people to Christ and He alone conquers the natural resistance of the sinner.
(3) Sovereign Regeneration and Security of the Elect: The Father saves infallibly all whom He draws, and preserves them until the resurrection of the Just. [3]

2. *John 17:*

This High Priestly prayer of Jesus reveals the intentions of the Father in sending Him to earth. What precisely were those intentions? Did Christ fulfill them in part, or totally?

Verse 2: Christ has power over all flesh. This shows that human flesh is unable to resist His saving power. According to the will of the Father, Christ gives eternal life to those the Father has given to Him. This chapter repeats seven times the key phrase, *"those you gave me."*

Verse 4: Christ completed the work the Father gave Him. Some believers have asked, "Why didn't Christ save the entire world?" If this had been the work that the Father had committed to Him, He would have accomplished it.

Verse 6: Christ revealed the Father only to those the Father had given Him.

Verse 9: If Christ had come to save the entire world, He

would have prayed for the entire world. Yet He prayed for the elect only.

Verse 11: Christ pleaded that the Father would preserve those the Father had given Him. Does the Father answer the prayers of Jesus? According to John 11:41, He does.

Verse 12: None of those whom Christ keeps are lost. He keeps those whom the Father gives to Him. Was he referring to the twelve disciples only? Not according to verse 20.

Notice the private and particular love of God for the elect expressed in the following verses: They are kept from evil (v. 15), sanctified (v. 17), sent into the world (v. 18), united with God the Father (v. 21), given God's glory (v. 22), and will be with Christ forever (v. 24).

The Father loves the elect just as He loves His only Son (v. 23).

If we believe that the intercessory ministry of Christ is effectual, then we must also believe that the elect receive infallibly all the benefits for which Christ prayed. We are gifts of the Father to Christ. God sent Jesus to secure the salvation of those the Father gave Him. Christ provided a sure redemption by His death on the Cross and His ministry of intercession as High Priest. By His irresistible power, the Father draws the elect to Christ. He regenerates them and preserves them infallibly for His glory.

A Glorious Impossibility: Romans 8:32-34

Paul declares, without the slightest ambiguity, the impossibility that any for whom Christ died could be lost. Why? Because the cross was truly efficacious.

> *He who did not spare His own Son, but delivered Him up for us all, how shall He not with Him also freely give us all things? Who shall bring a charge against God's elect? It is God who justifies. Who*

> *is he who condemns? It is Christ who died, and*
> *furthermore is also risen, who is even at the right*
> *hand of God, who also makes intercession for us.*
> (Romans.8:32-34)

According to verse 32, the benefits of the sacrifice of Christ invariably reach those for whom He gave His life. The phrase, "us all" refers in context to all believers. It refers to those who are predestinated, called, and justified (v. 30), who receive God's favor (v. 31), who are the elect (v. 33), who are not condemned (v. 34), whom God loves and preserves. (v. 35-39). In verse 33, Paul shows that God accepts no accusations against His elect and justified people, because Christ died for them.Verse 34 teaches that it is impossible that any of those be condemned for whom Christ died, resurrected, and for whom He intercedes. This passage teaches that the doctrine of Particular Redemption is not a philosophical fantasy, nor the fruit of theological reasoning. Paul expounds it with the utmost clarity.

The Covenant of Grace: The Foundation of the Bible

Imagine ourselves standing in front of a house with the blueprint in hand. The house is lovely, with a logical structure. Everything is functional and normal. But strangely, the house does not correspond to the blueprint. The windows are different. The door is on the wrong side. Obviously the blueprint is for another house.

The New Testament fulfills the Old Testament "blueprint" of divine redemption. We can study redemption from two angles: By noting the pattern of Old Testament history, we can predict the sort of redemption we see in the New Testament. Or, by studying the New Testament, we could predict the general nature of Old Testament history.

Suppose biblical redemption were as follows: God intended to save everyone. So He sent Christ to die on the cross with the intention of saving them all. This created a Covenant of Grace for everyone, which they could enter by their free will. Upon believing, they would enter the covenant where they would have salvation guaranteed, if they continued contributing their good will and obedience.

Is this biblical redemption? If this is a valid possibility, then we ought to read in the Old Testament the following scenario: God loved all nations and wanted to enter into Covenant with them. So He sacrificed a lamb for all the nations so that they could enter into it by their free will. Then He sent prophets throughout the world, to the Romans, Chinese, Aztecs, etc., inviting them to enter His covenant. But the only people who wanted to enter were good-natured people known for their obedience to God. These were the "Jews."

Is this the plan of redemption we see typified in the Old Testament? We notice that all nations were lost in idolatry and depravity. Nevertheless, God chose a people by pure sovereign election. These were the Jews. He did this because of His grace alone, not because of their merits nor obedience foreseen in them. God entered into covenant with them. To ratify this Covenant, He instituted a lamb sacrifice. The lamb was intended for them only, not for any other nation. By this sacrifice, God made this elect people acceptable to Himself.

By this scenario, we can deduce the kind of redemption story that should be found in the New Testament. God has a people chosen by grace, without consideration of merits foreseen in them. God entered into covenant with His elect, and sent Christ to confirm it by the sacrifice of Himself. Thus, God saved all His elect.

Which of these two scenarios is biblical? Notice the clear order of events: First, God chose a people. He then made an eternal covenant with them. Finally, He provided a sacrifice to confirm it and sanctify His people. Since the cross of Christ confirmed the covenant made with the elect, it follows that the sacrifice was intended for the Elect in particular, and them only.

Election, Covenant, Sacrifice: This is biblical redemption. Does Christ confirm the covenant for some, or for all? Matthew 26:28 says, *"For this is My blood of the new covenant, which is shed for many for the remission of sins."* "Many" does not mean "all." The blood of Jesus was the *"blood of the new covenant."* If the elect alone participate in the covenant, and if Christ poured out His blood to confirm the covenant, then Christ died with the intent of saving the elect alone.

Hebrews 9:14-15 affirms,

> *how much more shall the blood of Christ, who through the eternal Spirit offered Himself without spot to God, cleanse your conscience from dead works to serve the living God? And for this reason He is the Mediator of the new covenant, by means of death, for the redemption of the transgressions under the first covenant, that those who are called may receive the promise of the eternal inheritance.*

Christ is the mediator of the new covenant for those called to it. (Note here the idea of effectual call.) His blood cleanses the conscience of these alone, and they receive the promise of an eternal inheritance. Both the power and the limitation involved in His sacrifice are clearly expressed here. He died to guarantee the cleansing of all those called to an eternal inheritance.

The Intercession of Christ as Our High Priest

The ministry of the Jewish priest involved two activities: (1) offering sacrifices for the sins of the people; and (2) interceding for them on the basis of the sacrifice offered.

An inseparable link existed, therefore, between the sacrifice offered and the persons for whom the priest interceded. He never interceded for anyone without first offering a sacrifice for him.

Suppose we could transport ourselves to a time about twenty-eight hundred years ago and enter the temple of Jerusalem to watch the rituals performed. We notice a priest cutting the throat of a lamb in front of the altar. We ask him, "Priest, why are you killing this lamb?" The priest would answer, "Because I must approach the altar to intercede for a family that has sinned. The Lord will not allow me to approach without the blood of the lamb."

Immediately we understand that the lamb was sacrificed for this family. Suppose that we return the next day, but arrive late. The priest has already sacrificed the lamb and entered the temple to pray. We ask, "For whom was this lamb sacrificed? It looks like we'll never know because the priest has already entered the temple." Promptly, one of us suggests, "If we could hear the priest praying, we could deduce for whom the lamb was sacrificed." Quickly, we run around to the back side of tabernacle and put our ears to the wall. We hear the priest saying, "Lord, forgive the sins of the Josia family, and have mercy on them." Now we know for whom the lamb was slain, because the priest intercedes only for those for whom the sacrifice was made.

How does this relate to the ministry of our High Priest Jesus Christ? Let's listen again at the back wall. This time, we are not listening to a human priest, but to Christ Himself in His intercessory ministry.

I pray for them. I do not pray for the world but for those whom You have given Me, for they are Yours (John 17:9).

If Christ died with the intention of saving all, why isn't He praying for all? If He intercedes for some, then His sacrifice was intended for them alone.

Jesus, as our High Priest, performs both functions of the priesthood: sacrifice and intercession. Like the Priests of old, he fulfills these functions for the covenant people, and them alone. Thus, we read: *"The Lord has sworn And will not relent, 'You are a priest forever . . .' by so much more Jesus has become a surety of a better covenant"* (Hebrews 7:21-22).

Summary of Evidence

Theological reasoning is not the only evidence available to prove the particular nature of Christ's sacrifice. The Scriptures declare clearly that Christ came to save:

His people: *... and you shall call His name Jesus, for He will save His people from their sins* (Matthew 1:21).

His sheep: *...and I lay down my life for the sheep* (John 10:15).

His church: *...the church of God which He has purchased with His own blood* (Acts 20:28).

His elect: *Who shall bring a charge against God's elect? It is God who justifies* (Romans 8:32-33).

Those who participate in His covenant: *...He is the mediator of the new covenant, by means of death, ...that those who are called might receive the promise of the eternal inheritance* (Hebrews 9:15).

Those for whom Christ intercedes: *I pray for them. I do not pray for the world but for those whom You have given me out of the world for they are yours* (John 17:9).

<u>Those the Father gave to Christ</u>: *Of those whom you gave Me I have lost none* (John 18:9).

Logical Evidence

Since we know that some will be saved, and others will not, it follows that a limitation of some sort exists relative to the sacrifice of Christ. Otherwise, all would be saved. All evangelical Christians believe, therefore, in a "limited" Atonement. We differ on the question of exactly *how* it is limited.

The limitation could only involve one of two domains: Either the Cross is limited in its *power*, or it is limited in its *intention*. If we say it is limited in its *power*, then we declare that there is only enough power to save a limited number. (We can discard this option right away in the face of many texts expressing the power of the Cross.) If it is limited in its *intention*, then it was designed to save certain people, although it may have the power to redeem more.

The key question, though, is whether the cross depends on some cooperation from man to make it efficacious. We have already seen that man contributes nothing at all to his salvation. Even the exercise of his faith and free will is the result of divine grace.

This forces us to a conclusion: The efficacy of the cross depends on itself alone, not on the cooperative actions of man. We cannot have it both ways. If the power of the cross depends on the cooperative work of man, then it is not a *completed* sacrifice. Conversely, if the cross is truly *efficacious*, then it will produce the requisite cooperative actions in those for whom it is intended.

If the benefits of the Cross come infallibly to those for whom Christ was given, then it was for them alone. This sacrifice is worthy of trust because it guarantees a complete work of sanctification.

How Should The Message Of The Cross Be Preached?

In 1 Corinthians 2:2 we read, *"For I determined not to know anything among you except Jesus Christ and Him crucified."* A dilemma presents itself for those who come to understand the doctrine of the efficacious sacrifice of Christ. They feel restricted from saying to an unbeliever, "Christ died for you.' And they are right. In one sense, this is restrictive. If we cannot say this, what then *should* we say? The theologian, J.I. Packer, notes this tension:

> "We want (rightly) to proclaim Christ as Savior; yet we end up saying that Christ, having made salvation possible, has left us to become our own saviours. It comes about in this way. We want to magnify the saving grace of God and the saving power of Christ. So we declare that God's redeeming love extends to every man, and that Christ has died to save every man, and we proclaim that the glory of divine mercy is to be measured by these facts. And then, in order to avoid universalism, we have to depreciate all that we were previously extolling, and to explain that, after all, nothing that God and Christ have done can save us unless we add something to it; the decisive factor which actually saves us is our own believing. What we say comes to this- that Christ saves us with our help; and what that means, when one thinks it out is this- that we save ourselves with Christ's help. This is a hollow anti-climax. "[4]

The answer to this tension is a beautiful paradox. The

purpose of a clearer understanding of the cross is not to limit our preaching, but to free us to focus on the saving *power* of the Cross. This should have been our focus all along.

We tell people that the Cross saves *completely* and *surely* all who trust in Jesus.

We have in the Cross a sure salvation, a sovereign Savior who saves to the end, and initiates a reconciliation with an infinitely holy God. He pardons all our sins and incorporates us into an eternal covenant, via a Cross that preserves us forever. This is what the apostles preached.

On the other hand, the doctrine of universal atonement contains serious contradictions that can provoke a thoughtful person to reject the gospel. First, if Christ died with the intention of saving all, then He accomplished little more than a mere fraction of His intention. In this case, He is largely a failed Savior. Worse, He cannot save *me* unless I help Him by cooperating with my free will and evangelical obedience. This translates ultimately into saving oneself with a bit of help from a Savior who could only give it a shot and hope for the best. Why bother to trust in a Savior like that?

Second, it is contradictory to preach a powerful cross if it is man, not God, who makes it work. Third, it is impossible to preach a sovereign God unless He is able to fulfill His intentions. He could hardly be worshiped as wise if He undertook a purpose that He Himself never intended to complete.

Finally, no saved sinner would have security in salvation unless the gift of perseverance were a benefit purchased in the Cross. Salvation without security is a Gospel of merit, which is precisely what universal atonement leads to. An intelligent unbeliever, upon hearing that Christ died to save all, but that few will be saved, would conclude instantly that he is not hearing about a sovereign Savior. He would understand that such a Cross has no power to save or preserve anybody. Fortunately, most are not so thoughtful. By God's grace, ironically, they *miss* the contradictions in modern preaching.

When we preach the Cross, let's declare a totally efficacious Savior. His Cross guarantees a sure salvation for every believer. It is the certainty of a future perfection. We can explain that the final words of Jesus, "It is finished," mean a complete salvation to which nothing can be added. All is of grace.

Questions Regarding the Sacrifice of Christ

1. The concept of "propitiation" for "the whole world" is apparently proclaimed in *1 John 2:2: "And He Himself is the propitiation for our sins, and not for ours only but also for the whole world."* Doesn't this refute the idea of a sacrifice limited to the elect?

Answer: This verse is the bulwark of the doctrine of universal atonement. It supposedly explains that the death of Christ expiates not only the sins of Christians, but also those of all the lost. It is said that the word "our" refers to all Christians and the word "the whole world" refers to all the lost. Whether this view is correct depends on the common sense rules of biblical interpretation. Two rules in particular apply here: Context and ordinary word usage.

First, let's give a clear definition of the key words used. The word "propitiation" signifies "appease wrath." The New Testament uses it five times to show that the wrath of God is appeased regarding sin. According to 1 John 2:2, the wrath of God is appeased with respect to somebody. It is now necessary to deduce who those persons are from the context.

Let's assume that God's wrath is appeased for everyone in the entire world. What then of the hundreds of verses that announce the wrath of God toward sinners? What of the book of Revelation, which depicts His wrath to be poured out on the whole world? The Cross apparently did not appease the wrath of God toward the entire world, because if it did, nobody would be condemned.

The word "propitiation" in Ro. 3:25 expresses appeasement only for those justified by faith in Christ. In 1 John .2: 2, the Apostle declares that God's wrath is appeased toward those brothers to whom he is writing, and toward all other believers throughout the world. If God is angry with no one, then we are forced to the conclusion that all are saved.

Second, who are the brothers to whom John is writing? This Epistle is directed to Jewish Christians since John was an Apostle to the Jews. We read in 2:7 of a divine commandment that the hearers had received "from the beginning." Only Jews, not Gentiles, had received commandments from God. The Book of Acts reveals that first-century Jewish Christians tended to forget that the Gentile believers were accepted in Christ equally with them. Their Jewish background led them to feel superior. John, in this epistle, tells them that Christ died for the scattered brethren in the whole world, not just for believing Jews.

Below is a study of the words, "world" and "whole world," to show that they do not normally mean "all of humanity."

> Believers in the world: Luke 2:1; John 12:19.
> Unbelievers in the world: John 15:18, 16:20, 17:14;
> 2 Peter 2:5; 1 John 5:19; Revelation 10, 13:3, 16:14.
> The Universe: Acts 17:24
> People of all ethnic groups in the world: John 1:10, 29.
> The general public: John 7:4, 12:19, 14:22.

Of the 105 times that John uses the word "world" in his writings, only eleven times does it mean every human being. Even in those eleven cases, such an interpretation is doubtful. The basic rule for interpreting biblical words is this: The meaning of a word is determined by its most frequent usage, unless the context shows the need for another meaning.

2. Certain texts use the word "all," in reference to the sacrifice of Christ. For example, 1 Timothy 2:4-6 says, *"who desires all men to be saved and to come to the knowledge of the truth. For there is one God and one Mediator between God and men, the Man Christ Jesus, who gave Himself a ransom for all, to be testified in due time."* Similar usage is found in Hebrews 2:9 and 2 Corinthians 5:14-15. How does this correspond with the idea of an atonement limited to the elect?

<u>Answer:</u> We have already affirmed the hypothetical sufficiency of the Cross for all mankind. The only point we have denied is that the divine intention in sending Christ was to save all. Nevertheless, it is easy to show that the phrase, "all" and "all men," in these texts, does not mean all humanity without exception of person. Let us focus principally on 1 Timothy 2:4-6 because the same arguments that apply to this text apply to the similar ones also:

The words "all men" in this context means all without distinction of *class or race*, not "all" without exception of *person*. The context, along with a brief study of this phrase throughout the Bible, confirms this. This phrase "all men" appears hundreds of times in the Bible. In less than ten percent of the cases can it mean "every person that has ever existed." Normally it means "all sorts of people."

One example is found in Titus 2:11: *"For the grace of God that brings salvation has appeared to all men."* At the time Paul wrote this, the grace of God had not been manifested to everyone in the world. Is Paul exaggerating? No. He is simply saying that the Gospel is universal, and that it transcends the limits of culture and race. God has elect people among the nations also, not only among the Jews.

Another example is found in Acts 2:17: *"I will pour out my Spirit on all flesh."* On the day of Pentecost, only a few people received the Spirit. People of all *kinds* are mentioned here, without distinctions of ages or social standing.

Is there something in 1 Timothy that would lead us to ignore 90% of the biblical evidence concerning the use of the phrase "all men"? The context shows narrow limitations as to 1 Tim 2:4-6. Notice verses 1-2: *"... prayers...for kings and all who are in authority."* Paul mentions specifically the civil authorities. The gospel must be preached even to pagan rulers, and prayer offered for them, because God may have Elect even among them. In verse 7, Paul shows that he has in mind the Gentiles also when he says, "all men." The message of Chapter 2 is that God wishes to save people of all kinds, Gentiles as well as Jews, and rulers as well as the poor. Nothing in this text, therefore, teaches universal atonement.

Below follows a brief study on the biblical usage of the terms "all" and "all men."

All believers: Acts 2:45, 17:31; Romans 16:19; 1 Corinthians 7:7; 3 John 12.

All unbelievers: Luke 21:17; 2 Timothy 4:16; Revelation 19:18.

People of every class (i.e., people without exception of class, but not without exception of person.): Mark 1:37; Luke 3:15; John 3:26; 13:35; Acts 2:17; 21:28; 2 Corinthians 3:2; 2 Timothy 4:16; Titus 2:11.

Everyone present: Mark 5:20; Acts 4:21, 20:19, 20:26

3. If limited atonement is the correct doctrine, then isn't God insincere in offering salvation to all based on the sacrifice of Jesus?

<u>Answer:</u> We have clearly asserted that the cross of Christ is sufficient to save any number of sinners. Therefore, on the grounds of this sufficiency, it is not contradictory for God to offer salvation to all.

Speaking hypothetically, would God forgive a reprobate on the grounds of Christ's sacrifice, were he to come to Christ. Yes! The *sufficiency* of the Cross shows that the barrier in coming to Christ resides entirely in the sinner. God never built a wall between Himself and any man. The wall is in man's own nature, not God's.

Further, the question above contains a hidden presupposition that deserves careful examination. The assumption is that the gospel is *primarily* an offer of salvation. We heartily agree that it is an *offer*. We may, however, question if the offer is the foremost consideration. Let's look at a common element in the gospel as preached by prominent biblical figures:

Mark 1:15: *"Repent, and believe in the gospel."*

Luke 24:47: *"and that repentance and remission of sins should be preached in His name to all nations, beginning at Jerusalem."*

Acts 3:19: *"Repent therefore and be converted, that your sins may be blotted out."*

Acts 17:30: *"Truly, these times of ignorance God overlooked, but now commands all men everywhere to repent."*

Acts 20:21: *"testifying to Jews, and also to Greeks, repentance toward God and faith toward our Lord Jesus Christ."*

What is central in these verses? *Repentance.* Now let's

ask, "if Christ never came and died for anybody at all, would God still require repentance?" Absolutely! God's holiness must be vindicated above all. In the creature-Creator relationship, rebellious subjects owe repentance despite any other considerations.

The call to repentance is inherent in the Gospel. Therefore, it makes sense to offer the Gospel to all mankind. Inherent in this call is the assumption that God will accept the repentance of any sinner. Why a reprobate does not repent is another subject. To show that God is insincere in offering the Gospel to all mankind, it would be necessary to prove that God would not accept such repentance. Nothing in the doctrine of limited atonement suggests this.

Review Questions

1. True or False: _____The death of Christ accomplished all the conditions of salvation for the elect, except faith and obedience.

2. Other names for our doctrine are _____ or _____.

3. Universal atonement means that Christ died for: (Mark One)
   A. The Elect only
   B. All of humanity

4. Limited atonement means that Christ died for: (Mark One)
   A. The Elect only
   B. All of humanity

5. Explain in your own words why this doctrine is important:

6. True or False: _____Conversion to Christ means that God changes "goats" to "sheep."

7. Christ came to give his life for the _____, according to John 10.

8. How does Christ transfer His life to the sheep?

_____

9. True or False: _____A believer's faith is a *result* of being a sheep, not the *cause* of being a sheep.

10. True or False: _____We make ourselves the Lord's sheep by receiving eternal life.

11. We become the Lord's sheep by: (Mark One)
      A. A decision of our free will.
      B. By our faith in Christ.
      C. By an eternal decree of God the Father in giving us to Christ.

12. The key phrase for understanding the Gospel of John is:

_____

13. True or False: _____We belong to God the Father by a divine decree before belonging to Christ.

14. An analysis of John 6:37-45, 65 revealed to us certain important truths. These are:

A.

B.

C.

15. Which of the doctrines of grace are proven by John 6:44:

16. In which chapter of the Bible is found the high-priestly prayer of Christ before He went to the Cross?

17. According to John 17, to whom does Christ give eternal life?

18. Christ accomplished: (Choose One)
   A. All the work the Father gave Him to do.
   B. Part of the work the Father gave Him to do.
   C. Whatever He could, according to the ability of man to the cooperation he could get from people.

19. When Christ said that He preserves all those the Father has given to Him, He is talking about: (Mark One)
   A. The Twelve Disciples only.
   B. Believers of all epochs of history.
   C. Those who keep themselves faithful by the power of their free will.

20. The great impossiblity that Paul expresses in Ro. 8:32-34 consists in that _____

21. In Romans 8:33, Paul shows that God does not receive accusations against His elect and justified people because: (Mark One)
    A. God only justifies those whom He knows beforehand are going to be faithful.
    B. Christ died for them.
    C. They are worthy.

22. True or False: _____Our doctrine is the product of theological reasoning only and not because they are clearly expressed in the Bible.

23. The biblical pattern of redemption follows three specific steps in the two Testaments. These are:

24. For whom is Christ Mediator of the New Covenant according to Hebrews 9: 14-15? _____

25. The two aspects of Christ's priestly ministry, along with the Jewish priests in the Old Testament are:
    A.

    B.

26. True or False: _____As a faithful High Priest, Christ intercedes only for those for whom He made sacrifice.

27. True or False: _____Christ interceded for the salvation of the world.

28. Fill the following blank spaces:
    A. According to Matthew 1:21, Christ died for

    _____.

    B. According to John 10:15, Christ died for

    _____.

    C. According to Ephesianws 5:25, Christ died for

    _____.

    D. According to Hebrews 9:15 Christ died for

    _____.

    E. According to John 17:9 Christ intercedes for

    _____.

29. The logical conclusion of the doctrine of universal atonement, if it were true, is that

30. If all humanity is not going to be saved, then we must conclude that the Cross had one of two limitations: (Mark One)
    A. Limited in its efficacity.
    B. Limited in the extent of its intention.

31. The word "propitiation" means _____

32. The correct interpretation of 1 John 2:2 is: (Mark One)
    A. Christ appeased the wrath of God toward all of humanity.
    B. Christ appeased the wrath of God toward all believers through the whole world.
    C. Christ did not appease the wrath of God toward anyone.

33. True or False: _____The words "world," and "the whole

world" in the Bible, normally refers to the entire human race.

34. In the Bible, the words "all" and "all men" normally mean:
    A. Every human being which has existed.
    B. Every kind of human being.
    C. All Gentiles but not all Jews.

35. True or False: _____The doctrine of universal atonement contains more limitations than the doctrine of limited atonement.

Notes:

1. Packer, J.I.: Introductory Essay to: *Death of Death* by John Owen, Banner of Truth Trust, pp.10.

2. Ibid

3. Some have affirmed that the word "draw" in this verse suggests a moral persuasion that the sinner can resist. The problem with this interpretation is that the Greek word "draw" used here,(HELKUO), always means drag, in the sense of compulsion. Even if we did not know what it meant, we could deduce its meaning from the phrase, "and I will raise him up at the last day." That is to say, all those who are objects of the Father's drawing action will be saved infallibly. This leaves no room for an effective resistance by the sinner.

4. Packer, J.I.: Introductory essay to *Death of Death* by John Owen, Banner of Truth Trust, pp.14.

Chapter Summary — Sacrifice of Christ

From this chapter on the Sacrifice of Christ we learned that:

1. Christ's death guaranteed the salvation of all the elect and those only.
2. Christ came to save those given to Him by the Father, the elect, and those only. He succeeded 100% in this task.
3. All Christians believe in a limited atonement. The question is 'where is the limitation?'
4. While the sacrifice of Christ is sufficient to save any number of sinners, it was not intended for all.
5. All of the conditions for salvation that man must fulfill to obtain the benefits of salvation are also provided in the cross, including saving faith. The benefits include justification, sanctification, eternal life, perfection, forgiveness, sealing with the Holy Spirit and more. These benefits are guaranteed only for the elect.
6. The Bible clearly teaches that it is impossible for those for whom Christ died to perish. Rom.8:30-39.
7. The intercessory ministry of Christ as High Priest proves He died for the elect because He interceded for them only. Jn.17
8. We preach the power of the cross rather than its extent because that is how the Apostles preached.

Chapter Six
Unity and Universality of the Church

"Which is the true church?" We hear this question occasionally when we testify about Christ. Some churches, especially cults, declare themselves the only true one, outside of which salvation is impossible. The Bible reveals something surprising about this issue. The church that Christ founded is an invisible organism, not a visible organization. Its structure is spiritual, not material. So, being a member of a religious organization of any kind is no guarantee that one belongs to Christ's church. Conversely, it is possible to be a member of a local church that does not belong to Christ at all. All this can appear confusing until we analyze what we mean by the unity and universality of the Church.

Who Belongs to the True Church?

The Church of Christ consists of all those saved by faith in Christ. In Acts 2:47 we read, *"And the Lord added to the church daily those who were being saved."* So it is plain that only those saved are part of the true church of Christ. In I Corinthians 1: 2 we read, *"To the church of God which is at Corinth, to those who are sanctified in Christ Jesus, called to be saints, with all who in every place call on the name of Jesus Christ our Lord, both theirs and ours."* According to this text, God's church consists of people who are sanctified in Christ, called by God to a holy life, pray in the name of the Lord Jesus, and recognize His Lordship. This is distinct from an occasional attendance at meetings coupled with a few religious practices.

Viewing it this way, we can say without hesitation, that some members of Christ's body belong to churches that are not biblical. Others may attend true churches that preach the Gospel, without belonging to Christ at all. Not all who participate in meetings are necessarily regenerate. Some participate by custom or culture without ever knowing the Lord.

Jesus said in John 17 that those who belong to Him have eternal life (v. 2), know God (v. 3), receive God's Words (v. 8), are hated by the world (v. 16), are sanctified (v. 17), and are united in love (v. 21-23). These alone will be with Him in glory. The universal character of the Church is seen in the words of Jesus in John 10:16: *"And other sheep I have which are not of this fold; them also I must bring, and they will hear My voice; and there will be one flock and one shepherd."*

The Jews believed that they alone were objects of salvation. But here, Jesus reveals that He has other sheep besides the Jews and that they all form one sheepfold. His sheep have faith in Him, (v. 26), hear His voice (v. 27), and follow Him (v. 27). The Father preserves them unfailingly, so that none are lost (vv. 28-29).

Organization or Organism?

In Ephesians 4:11-12 we read, *"And He Himself gave some to be apostles, some prophets, some evangelists, and some pastors and teachers, for the equipping of the saints for the work of ministry, for the edifying of the body of Christ, till we all come to the unity of the faith and of the knowledge of the Son of God, to a perfect man, to the measure of the stature of the fullness of Christ."*

The Church of Christ has officials. These are apostles, prophets (preachers), evangelists, pastors and teachers. (v. 11) Their job is to prepare Christians to minister to humanity, to unite believers in the faith, and bring them into a deeper knowledge of the Lord Jesus Christ. (vv. 12-13)

Though Christ's church has officials, it would be a mistake to suppose that is principally an organization. The following verses express a supremely important truth: His church is primarily an organism, not an organization. It is a "body," of which Christ is the head (vv. 15-16). No one but Christ has the right to take to himself the title of "head" of the Church.

What Should the Body of Christ Look Like On the Local Scene?

In a legal sense, God perceives the universal church as united in Christ, justified and acceptable before the Father. Nevertheless, the body of Christ has visible manifestations as local churches. All these lack perfection to some degree. Some have such serious defects in doctrine and organization that we might ask ourselves if they qualify as legitimate expressions of our Lord's church. Although we would like to avoid a critical attitude, it is necessary to have clear criteria to help us distinguish between legitimate churches and false ones.

The Word of God gives us such criteria, and we are going to study it now. Though some churches may be more mature than others, all should strive for the biblical ideal if they wish to be considered as a legitimate part of the body of Christ. We have organized these criteria below according to four divisions to simplify their study: Purity of doctrine, of organization, of behavior, and of worship.

I. Purity of Doctrine

Doctrinal differences on minor points will always exist among Christians. These include the mode of baptism, the best way to hold services, etc. However, certain doctrines are central to biblical doctrine and therefore essential. A denial of any of these is grounds for declaring a church doctrinally impure, without the right to call itself a part of the body of Christ.

These essential doctrines are: The infallibility of the Bible as the Word of God, and as sufficient for all questions of doctrine and practice; the Holy Trinity; the Deity of Christ, His virgin birth, His death and bodily resurrection and His second coming; Salvation by grace without merits; eternal judgment for sinners and eternal happiness for believers. [1]
If a Christian finds himself in a church that denies any of these doctrines, he should separate from it immediately. Though "good" people may attend it, God disapproves of it because it denies essential truths revealed in His Word.

II. Purity of Organization
A legitimate body of believers recognizes Jesus Christ as the only head of the universal church. It rejects all authorities, whether civil or religious, who claim the right to govern all Christians on earth.

It practices a plurality of elders (Acts 14:23; Titus 1:5). The elders are spiritual leaders of the church, such as pastors, evangelists and missionaries (Ephesians 4: 11-12), who govern with authority without being authoritarian (1 Peter 5:1-3). They pastor the church and take care of it spiritually (Acts 20:28). One man alone must not govern the church as dictator or supreme authority. Those who rule *anything* without accountability can easily become abusive. Such a church is profoundly impure in the organizational sense.[2]

Final authority in the church resides with the elders, not with the congregation. The kingdom of God is not a democracy. God governs it through the elders and not by congregational voting. The elder, not the congregation, is God's agent (Acts. 20:28; 1 Thessalonians 5:12-13; Hebrews 13:17).

The local church has no authority to decide for itself

what is sound doctrine. Church Councils resolve theological difficulties. These consist of all the elders and missionaries associated with the same organization of churches. Such Councils then implemrnt the decrees in the local churches (Acts 15:1-31; 16:4). For example, in the first-century controversy over circumcision, the early Christians did not appeal to some ecclesiastical authority to decree what was correct. Nor did they leave it to each congregation to decide for itself. Nor did they decide that truth is merely a matter of personal conscience, nor that each Christian has the right to his own opinion. A certain amount of liberty of conscience on minor issues is acceptable. However, on major matters, such as those touching on the means of salvation, the early Christians handed down decrees based on the deliberations of the Council of elders (Acts 15).

In the daily life of the church, the elders labor in doctrine and teaching, maintaining the standards of sound doctrine. Controversial questions that cannot be resolved by the creeds of the church become the prerogative of the council of elders.

Although some evangelical churches lack organizational purity, this is insufficient reason to separate oneself from them. Some have received no instruction about biblical government, but serve the Lord with a sincere heart. Organizational questions are less important than doctrinal or moral ones. If, however, the conduct of the leaders is authoritarian to the point that the spiritual development of the believer is hindered, then it may be legitimate to search for another church. Similarly, if the leaders fail to exercise biblical discipline to the point that impurity runs rampant in the church, then it may be time to separate.

III. Purity of Testimony

A Biblical church exercises moral discipline. The elders

counsel members who persist in serious sin, or place them under discipline according to the case. Those who refuse the counsel of the elders and persist in sin, must be excommunicated. The biblical church must not have a bad reputation in the community as tolerant of serious sin (Ephesians 5:13).

The biblical church practices separation from the world. Legitimate churches have no fellowship or cooperation with religious organizations which fail to maintain sound doctrine or which practice idolatry. Unity without truth is nothing more than an ungodly union (2 Corinthians 6:14-18).

The biblical church does not practice legalism. Rather, it preaches righteousness based on faith in Christ alone, not in exterior matters such as clothing, types of food, or Sabbath observances (Galatians 3:1-6; Colossians 2:16).

The biblical church evangelizes. It is contradictory for a church to consider itself biblical, if it does not fulfill one of the major purposes for its existence. The Great Commission of Jesus in Matthew 28:19 expresses that purpose: *"Go therefore and make disciples of all the nations."*

IV. Purity of Worship

The Word of God must be preached and taught faithfully – not social activism, nor political theories, nor human philosophies nor private opinions (2 Timothy 4:1-2).

The ordinances of baptism and the Lord's supper are administered faithfully, and not neglected (Acts 2:42).

Order exists in the services. Noise and disorder are not found there (1 Corinthians 14:23, 40). Note: New churches are in the process of development, and have lacked the time to develop these points. This is tolerable. However, those that previously knew the truth, but have veered from biblical standards, are without excuse.

The Corinthian church was carnal, out of order and immoral. Nevertheless, Paul called it "the church of God."

Why did he do this when the church was in such a deplorable condition? He knew they were "babes" in Christ, and lacked teaching. They had come out of a pagan culture, and lacked understanding. Would it have been legitimate for a believer to separate from such a church? No. It is better to remain and help the membership move toward maturity. Withdrawal is justified only if the church refuses to progress toward godly standards.

Important Questions About The Church
1. Are denominations legitimate?

This question is double-sided. Division among Christians is a clear sign of carnality and spiritual immaturity. In a certain sense, denominationalism contributes to division by tempting Christians to adopt exclusivist attitudes. Some imagine that their denomination is spiritually superior to all others. They feel sorry for Christians who belong to other denominations, and their conscience bothers them little if they steal "sheep" from legitimate churches.

Yet denominations have played a profoundly beneficial role. With false cults proliferating, it seems reasonable for a group of churches to associate to maintain their purity. Moreover, a presbytery could hardly exist, nor a council of churches, unless a denomination exists first. (The idea of presbyteries and councils is biblical. See 1 Timothy 4:14 and Acts 15). If the best way to maintain a biblical system of government is through a denomination, then it is perfectly legitimate.

2. Who has the right to exercise discipline in the church?

The spiritual leaders fulfill this function according to Galatians 6:1:

Brethren, if a man is overtaken in any trespass, you who

are spiritual restore such a one in a spirit of gentleness, considering yourself lest you also be tempted.

3. What are legitimate reasons for excommunion?

Provoking divisions, (Titus 3:10); heresy, (Romans 16:17); and persistence in serious sin (1 Corinthians 5:9-13).

Summary

The true church of Christ is a living organism, formed by all those saved by faith in Jesus Christ. He alone is head of church. The essential nature of the church is supernatural, not of human origin. In its local expression, the church of Christ exhibits purity in doctrine, organization, behavior and worship.

Review Questions

1. True or False: _____The church of Christ as no kind of organization.

2. True or False: _____The church of Christ is primarily an organism and not an organization.

3. True or False: _____The church of Christ has one head, the Pope.

4. True or False: _____Those who are saved, and those only, are part of the universal church of Christ.

5. True or False: _____ Some Catholics may be part of the Body of Christ, while some Protestants may not.

6. True or False: _____ The church of Christ, in the universal sense, is a visible organism.

7. True or False: _____ The church of Christ is principally a spiritual entity, not a terrestrial one.

8. True or False: _____ Being a member of a local church that preaches the Bible guarantees personal salvation.

9. True or False: _____ All churches that call themselves Christian are legitimate expressions of the universal body of Christ.

10. True or False: _____ Legitimate churches always fulfill all the biblical criteria mentioned in this study.

11. The four basic divisions of biblical criteria mentioned in this study are, purity of _____, _____, _____, _____.

12. True or False: _____ To be correctly organized, a local church must have plurality of elders.

13. True or False: _____ "Elders" means the elderly gentlemen of the church.

14. True or False: _____ The Bible indicates that presbyteries and councils are legitimate.

15. True or False: _____ The Council (or Presbytery) consists of all the elders who belong to a body of associated churches.

16. True or False: _____ In the local church, it is the spiritual leaders who have authority to exercise spiritual discipline.

17. True or False: _____According to the democratic ideal of the Bible, a local congregation has the authority to decide for itself what is sound doctrine.

18. True or False: _____If a local church is not perfectly organized, the Christian has the right to separate from it immediately.

19. True or False: _____It is right for churches to participate in ecumenical movements with churches that do not maintain sound doctrine, to display a spirit of tolerance.

20. True or False: _____ In our era, it is proper that the pulpit may be used for social activism.

Notes:
1.   In other words, the contents of the Apostle's Creed.
2.   The ancient dictum, 'absolute power corrupts absolutely', is as true in a church as anywhere else. Sometimes I think it is more so.

Chapter Summary — Unity of the Church
From this chapter on the Unity of the Church, we learned that:

1. The church of Christ consists of all those saved by faith in Christ, that is, the elect.
2. The church is essentially an organism, not an organization.
3. The church of Christ is revealed in its local manifestations by its purity in doctrine, organization testimony and worship
4. Authority in Christ's church rests with the ordained leaders called 'elders', not with the congregation via democratic voting. The church is not a democracy.

Chapter Seven

Security of the Believer

Mr. Jones lived a life of unabashed perversity until the day he attended an evangelistic meeting. There he responded to the "invitation" to accept Christ and make a public profession of faith. During the following months he dutifully attended the discipleship meetings, read the Bible, and showed definite improvements in his conduct.

But one day he turned up drunk on the street. During the following weeks, various Christians tried to help him, but he refused all counsel. He returned to his old ways and vehemently denied the Gospel. He remained in this state for several years and afterwards died. Did Mr. Jones go to heaven or hell?

For generations, Christians have discussed this vital issue: "Can a Christian lose his salvation?" In the sixteenth century, a certain religious party[1] raised this question and insisted that born-again Christians could lose their salvation by persisting in serious sins or apostatizing from the faith. Members of that religious party would affirm that Mr. Jones is in hell. Others rejected their view and said that "Christians" such as Mr. Jones would go to heaven despite their apostasy because they were once born again.[2]

The first party said that their doctrine was necessary to put the fear of God into Christians; otherwise they would have a license to sin. The others insisted that only a doctrine of absolute security could avoid contaminating the gospel with a philosophy of salvation by merit.

Fortunately, these two viewpoints are not the only options. Another exists, clearly taught by the Reformers. (The other two views are actually perversions of the original Reformation teaching.) This doctrine is called "the perseverance and preservation of the elect."[3]

A definition of the doctrine of preservation can be stated as follows: God has an elect and justified people whom He preserves from a life of sin, and from ultimately apostatizing from the faith so as to lose their salvation. He accomplishes this by His grace, through the Holy Spirit and His Word.

Let's notice that this definition differs radically from important points in the other two views. First, our preservation is linked intimately with two other important doctrines, election and justification. Second, the doctrine asserts that certain conditions exist by which a Christian would lose his salvation **if** God permitted him to fulfill them. These are: living a life of sin, and apostatizing from the faith. In this sense, preservation agrees with the first party – at least hypothetically. It differs in that God preserves His people from apostatizing, since the basis of preservation is the Cross, not human effort.

Third, the doctrine affirms that the elect do not lose their salvation. In this sense it agrees with the second view, but differs in two important particulars: It denies the possibility that God would allow an elect person to apostatize ultimately and finally. It also grounds the preservation in the doctrines of election and justification, rather than in the idea of being born-again. This again, takes the preservation out of the domain of human abilities and puts it into the dimension of God's decrees.

Finally, though preservation may be a gift of grace, it

operates by practical means which have to do with Christian living as a whole. Ironically, the other two viewpoints, while seeming exact opposites, have something crucial in common: Both are rooted in something that man thinks or does.

Misunderstandings are easy at this point. To clarify, let's see precisely what the doctrine of preservation does *not* mean. It does not mean that Christians have a license to sin. God preserves His people from acting in such a manner. The ground of our security of salvation is God's ability to preserve us from conditions that might result in losing our salvation.

Nor does the doctrine affirm that Christians are alleviated from the responsibility to apply the necessary means for their own preservation. God knows how to make life uncomfortable for negligent believers.

Nor does preservation mean that God deprives His people of their freedom of will. We affirm that God's people can apostatize if they wish. How God employs means to ensure that they will never wish to do so is the subject of the next section.

The Biblical Evidence

If election is true, then preservation must be true. To be chosen from eternity implies that God will use whatever means necessary to ensure that the elect attain the goal for which He created them. Although the logic involved is sufficient verification, nevertheless, the Scriptures themselves affirm it by associating election with preservation in many New Testament texts:

1. Romans 8:30 teaches that our glorification is the final fruit of predestination. *"Moreover whom He predestined, these He also called; whom He called, these He also justified; and whom He justified, these He also glorified."*

2. John greets the *"elect lady and her children, whom I love in truth"* in 2 John 1-2 and then declares that the truth *"will be with us forever."*

3. According to Jude, the *"called"* are sanctified in God the Father and preserved in Jesus Christ." (v.1)

4. Ephesians 2:10 teaches that the good works of the elect are just as predestinated as the elect themselves. We must never forget this in any discussion of preservation. *"For we are His workmanship, created in Christ Jesus for good works, which God prepared beforehand that we should walk in them."*

5. Isaiah observed that all the good deeds that the people of God do are works that God has done in them. *"LORD, You will establish peace for us, For You have also done all our works in us."* (26:12). If the good works of the Elect are predestined by the Lord Himself, how could they do works that would condemn them?

If justification is true, so is preservation. Here, the imputation of the righteousness of Christ plays a vital role. If the righteousness of Christ is apart from merits, then our demerits cannot be a cause of its removal. If it is not our righteousness to start with, then neither is it ours to change. Our degree of sanctification may change, but not our justification. The latter is grounded in a divine decree, not in a merit of man.

No doctrine of de-justification is found in the Bible. Never does the Bible teach that a justified person can return to an unjustified state. That is why Paul says that God does not accept accusations against His elect and justified people. *"Who shall bring a charge against God's elect? It is God who justifies"* (Romans 8:32).

Does God simply ignore the sins of His people? No! In Romans 8, Paul refers to final condemnation. The first verse of the chapter introduces the principle theme, *"There is therefore now no condemnation to those who are in Christ Jesus."* Paul never teaches that Christians cannot sin – only that sin has ceased to be a cause of condemnation for the Christian. The remainder of Romans 8 is a description of what the elect are like. They do not live according to the flesh, but according to the Spirit. They have the inward testimony of the Spirit with no desire to live a life of sin.

Let's be absolutely clear on this point: Paul is not stating conditions here, as though he were saying "do these things and you will be saved." If so, he would be contradicting himself since he just finished seven chapters showing why salvation is by grace alone.

Chapter 6 of Romans emphasizes the same. Paul points out the impossibility of sinful living now that we are dead to sin through justification. *What shall we say then? Shall we continue in sin that grace may abound? Certainly not! How shall we who died to sin live any longer in it?* (vv. 1-2) In the three previous chapters, Paul explained how justification works. Then in chapter 6, he explains how justified people really live. Even though they are not completely free from sin, it no longer reigns over them because they are dead to it. They are slaves to righteousness. How then could they fail to persevere?

A line of logic frequently pops up in discussions of Preservation. It goes like this:
Serious sin brings condemnation. Some Christians commit serious sin. Therefore, some Christians are condemned. Although it sounds rather convincing at first glance, it fails for several reasons. First, The Bible never teaches that only serious sins cause condemnation. All sin deserves condemnation. To be consistent with the above logic, we would have to say that all Christians are condemned, since all sin daily.

Yet a more serious error lurks in the above logic in that it ignores justification. The entire purpose of justification is to throw up a barrier between sin and condemnation. If justification failed in this, there would be no point in being justified. Christ imputes His righteousness to the believer precisely to form this impenetrable barricade between sin and condemnation.

So the first premise is weak. Sin does not always result in condemnation. For God's elect, it never brings condemnation, because God accepts no accusations against them.
Does this give Christians a license to sin? No, it gives them a license to struggle toward the goal of sanctification without the dread of an austere heavenly Father threatening to leave them if they fail to perform adequately.

Genuine Christians do not want a license to sin. According to the Bible, the news of their security causes them to want to persevere. This, ironically, is one of the signs of their election.

And everyone who has this hope in Him purifies himself, just as He is pure (1 John 3:3).

The Doctrines Of Grace All Imply Preservation

- If God is sovereign and all things exist because of His immutable will, then none of His intentions can be frustrated, including the salvation of His elect.

- If we are totally unable to save ourselves, then likewise, we are unable to preserve ourselves. God does both.

- If the sacrifice of Christ is truly efficacious and none of those for whom He died can perish, then His people will be preserved. How much more so, if Jesus intercedes for them as their High Priest? Is He not the surety and mediator of a new covenant made for them?

- The elect are united **in** the body of Christ. He cuts off none of His own members.

- Our sanctification and effectual calling are linked with our preservation, according to Jude: *Jude, a bondservant of Jesus Christ, and brother of James, To those who are called, sanctified by God the Father, and preserved in Jesus Christ* (v. 1).

Plain Texts As Evidence

2 Timothy 4:18: *And the Lord will deliver me from every evil work and preserve me for His heavenly kingdom. To Him be glory forever and ever. Amen!*

1 Peter 1:5: *who are kept by the power of God through faith for salvation ready to be revealed in the last time.*

1 John 5:18: *We know that whoever is born of God does not sin; but he who has been born of God keeps himself, and the wicked one does not touch him.*

Jude 1:1: *Jude, a bondservant of Jesus Christ, and brother of James, To those who are called, sanctified by God the Father, and preserved in Jesus Christ.*

Jude 1:24: *Now to Him who is able to keep you from stumbling, And to present you faultless Before the presence of His glory with exceeding joy,*

Psalm 97:10: *He preserves the souls of His saints.*

Evidence From Biblical Logic.

Doctrines contrary to preservation produce a gospel of salvation based on the will and works of man. The basic problem with these doctrines is that they assume salvation to be a cooperative work between God and man.

The Bible urges Christians to attain security in their salvation. This makes sense only if preservation is true. (2 Peter 1:10; Hebrews 6:11, 19; 10:22; 1 John 5:13)

The Scriptures speak of the "seal" of the Holy Spirit which believers receive. This seal is "until the day of redemption." (Ephesians 1:13; 2 Corinthians 1:22) What value would such a "seal" have if it can be broken?

God's faithfulness is the basis our obedience, not human ability. He promises to confirm us as faithful to the end so that we will be without reproach. 1 Corinthians 1 1:8: *who will also confirm you to the end, that you may be blameless in the day of our Lord Jesus Christ.* The faithfulness of God preserves us from all evil and establishes us. 2 Thessalonians 3:3: *But the Lord is faithful, who will establish you and guard you from the evil one.*

God's power keeps us. 1 Peter 1:5: *who are kept by the power of God through faith for salvation ready to be revealed in the last time.*

We can have complete confidence that God will complete in us the good work that He began. Philippians 1:6: *being confident of this very thing, that He who has begun a good work in you will complete it until the day of Jesus Christ.*

The will of the Father is the final word in Preservation. The Father wills that none of those He has given to Jesus may perish. John 6:39: *This is the will of the Father who sent Me, that of all He has given Me I should lose nothing, but should raise it up at the last day.*

Jesus confirmed and guaranteed this by declaring that none

of these has perished. John 18:9: *that the saying might be ful-filled which He spoke, "Of those whom You gave Me I have lost none.* The immutable will of the Father is the ground of our consolation. Hebrews 6:17 –18: *Thus God, determining to show more abundantly to the heirs of promise the immutability of His counsel, confirmed it by an oath, that by two immutable things, in which it is impossible for God to lie, we might have strong consolation, who have fled for refuge to lay hold of the hope set before us.*

Since the elect cannot be deceived, they will not fall away. Matthew 24:24: *For false christs and false prophets will rise and show great signs and wonders to deceive, if possible, even the elect.*

Our Preservation is no less certain than the efficacy of Christ's intercession for His people. His intercession saves us forever. Hebrews 7:25: *Therefore He is also able to save to the uttermost those who come to God through Him, since He always lives to make intercession for them.* Christ prays that our faith may not fail, and that the Father will preserve His own. Luke 22:32: *But I have prayed for you, that your faith should not fail; and when you have returned to Me, strengthen your brethren.* John 17:11: *Now I am no longer in the world, but these are in the world, and I come to You. Holy Father, keep through Your name those whom You have given Me, that they may be one as We are.*

The doctrine of sanctification implies preservation because our final sanctification is guaranteed. In a legal sense, we have been perfected forever by the sacrifice of Christ. Hebrews 10:10,14: *By that will we have been sanctified through the offering of the body of Jesus Christ once for all. For by one offering He has perfected forever those who are being sanctified.* God promises our entire sanctification. 1 Thessalonians 5:23 –24: *Now may the God of peace Himself sanctify you completely; and may your whole spirit, soul, and body be preserved blameless at the coming of our Lord Jesus Christ. He who calls you is faithful, who also will do it.*

If A Christian Were To Live A Life Of Sin, Would He Go To Heaven Anyway?

That is the crucial question when a discussion of pres-ervation arises. Let's lay out several other questions of the same sort to expose the nature of the question above:

> What does a square circle look like?
> What is the color blue when it is green?
> If a sinner were perfect, would he be saved?

All these questions are in the same category, including the one about Christians living a life of sin. They make no sense because they are self-contradictory. The idea of a lost saint is as absurd as a perfect sinner or a square circle. Remember "Mr. Jones" at the beginning of this chapter who was "born-again" and lived a life of sin? One view says he is in hell. Another view says he is in heaven. The biblical view says he never existed.

No answers exist for illogical questions. (This is a fun-damental law of logic.) The only proper reply to the question, *If a Christian were to live a life of sin, would he go to heaven?* , is "Stop talking nonsense!" Nothing could be clearer on this point than 1 John 3:9: *Whoever has been born of God does not sin, for His seed remains in him; and he cannot sin, because he has been born of God.*

According to John's theology, whoever is "born of God" cannot practice a life of sin. We know, of course, that this does not mean temporary lapses or single instances of sin. After all, John made it clear that anyone claiming to have no sin is a liar. (1 John 1:8) However, we have the Lord Jesus Christ as our advocate whenever we fall into sin.[4] John explains why the regenerate do not practice sin. Jesus pre-serves them. 1 John 5:18: *We know that whoever is born of God does not sin; but he who has been born of God keeps himself, and the wicked one does not touch him.*

Biblical writers sometimes employ a teaching device called "Hypothesis contrary to fact." Jesus Himself used this tactic in John 8:55 when He said, *"And if I say, 'I do not know Him,' I shall be a liar like you; but I do know Him and keep His word."* Under the condition stated, Jesus would have been a liar. A mere hypothetical condition could not make that a reality.

The Apostle Paul used a similar example in Romans 2:13, while discussing justification by the Law: *(for not the hearers of the law are just in the sight of God, but the doers of the law will be justified;* He makes it clear that if anyone were to keep the law, he would be justified. Did Paul really believe that people exist who had been justified that way? Certainly not. Throughout Romans, we learn that no one keeps the law, and therefore it justifies no one. Paul speaks hypothetically to illustrate a spiritual principle.

The question about the fate of the soul of a sinful believer is in the same category. Hypothetically speaking, we could say he would go to hell. But this is a hypothesis only and has no existence in reality, because God preserves His people.

In practice, how do genuine believers react when they hear about preservation? Do they take it as a license to sin? What does John say? *And everyone who has this hope in Him purifies himself, just as He is pure* (1 John 3:3). This good news leads believers to want to purify themselves. This is the answer for those who fear that preservation is a license to sin.

Are there people who try to take advantage of the grace of God and use preservation as a pretext to sin? Yes, Jude 4 describes such people:

For certain men have crept in unnoticed, who long ago were marked out for this condemnation, ungodly men, who turn the grace of our God into lewdness and deny the only Lord God and our Lord Jesus Christ.

Those who attempt to take advantage of the doctrine of preservation in order to live in corruption prove themselves to be reprobates.

How Does God Preserve His People?

One of the most frequent objections against preservation is based on biblical exhortations to persevere. Supposedly, a command to persevere implies the real possibility of some not persevering, and thus being lost. Hebrews is replete with warnings against falling away. Threats of imminent condemnation abound for those who apostatize. Since apostasy results in condemnation, this ought to be a real danger for the people of God. Otherwise, the threats are in vain.

The answer to this objection is involved with a paradox expressed in Jeremiah 32:40: *And I will make an everlasting covenant with them, that I will not turn away from doing them good; but I will put My fear in their hearts so that they will not depart from Me.* God preserves His covenant people by putting His fear in their hearts. Fear of what? Fear of God Himself. Fear of falling.

How does God accomplish this? By means of exhortations, threats, and admonitions. These very things are the means He employs to ensure the faithfulness of His people. According to the above verse, the eternal nature of the covenant makes it impossible for God to stop blessing His people. A key way He blesses them is by putting His fear in them, to ensure that the covenant relationship remains intact.

So, a paradox exists between the responsibility of the believer to obey, versus the divine activity in preservation.

God Himself guarantees the faithfulness of His elect. Paul expresses this paradox in Philippians 2:12-13: *Therefore, my beloved, as you have always obeyed, not as in my presence only, but now much more in my absence, work out your own salvation with fear and trembling; for it is God who works in you both to will and to do for His good pleasure.*

In the first part, Paul exhorts the church to work out their own salvation, as though this were up to them.[5] But we already know that fallen man is totally unable to promote his own salvation by any effort of will or work. God produces in them the willingness and the ability to obey. Here's the paradox: Born-again believers could apostatize if they wanted to. They never want to, though, because God Himself gives them better sense.

A good example of the same strategy occurs in evangelism when God threatens eternal condemnation on all those who refuse to repent. Is this threat insincere toward the elect? From the viewpoint of God's eternal decrees to save His elect, it seems so. Nevertheless, God uses this very threat as the means to provoke them to repent. Although repentance itself is a gift of grace, it comes via this threat. It's no contradiction therefore, to say that repentance is both a responsibility of man and a gift of God.

The doctrine of preservation is similar. God reveals to His people the extreme danger of apostasy, putting His fear in their hearts. The paradox lies in the use of this means to guarantee that the danger will never happen.

In Chapter Two, we learned that the existence of a command to do a thing never proves the ability to do it. The same with exhortations and threats toward falling away. A warning against apostasy proves nothing about whether this has happened to any Christian. It is impossible to prove from the Bible that any born-again believer has ever been eternally lost. So, warnings and exhortations against apostasy never constitute evidence against the doctrine of preservation.

The Problem Of False Faith: The Religious Unregenerate

How do we distinguish between those born again and those who simply seem to be? Some folks are good actors. Others are sincerely religious and think they are saved.

Even the Apostles had difficulty distinguishing between the genuine and the false from time to time. Some people live such a life of consecration to Christ, accompanied by such fruits of the Spirit, that doubting them is absurd. Others live in a gray area between light and darkness and we wonder if they are really saved.

The entire book of I John was written to address this issue. In it, John emphasizes that he wants us to have assurance of our salvation. This would make no sense if a doctrine like preservation were incorrect. He adds that he wants us to have a fullness of joy in the knowledge of this security. It does not come cheap though. He gives us criteria throughout the book to help us distinguish between true believers and those who fake it.

What are these criteria? How do those born of God really live? According to John, they are in fellowship with God and with the brethren whom they love. They remain faithful to the church. They do not live in sin. They overcome the world by faith. They are generous in helping with the needs of the believers and testify of their faith in Christ to the world.

Having a mouth full of religious words is not one of John's criteria. Jesus Himself put it this way in Matthew 7:21-23:

Not everyone who says to Me, "Lord, Lord" shall enter the kingdom of heaven, but he who does the will of My Father in heaven. Many will say to Me in that day,

"Lord, Lord, have we not prophesied in Your name, cast out demons in Your name, and done many wonders in Your name?" And then I will declare to them, "I never knew you; depart from Me, you who practice lawlessness!"

Christ will not say, "Depart from me you backsliders!" He said, "I *never* knew you." The religious people mentioned in this text did two things irrelevant to salvation, and failed to do two things that *are* relevant. They praised God saying, "Lord! Lord!" And they "prophesied" in His name and even did miracles. However, they neither lived godly lives, nor did the will of the Father. Their faith was phony. Without holy lives, their words and miracles counted for nothing.

Another example of phony faith was Simon the magician. In Acts 8, we learn that *"he believed and was baptized."* Later, Peter reproved him because he perceived that his heart was not "right in the sight of God." Simon had a type of superficial faith, but not a *saving* faith. He participated in the religious activities of God's people, even to the point of being baptized. But he was not regenerate.

James devoted part of the second chapter of his epistle to this question of false faith. Even the demons have a kind of "faith"(James 2:9). But it's not a *saving* faith. Genuine faith results in an obedient life that produces good works, such as the two examples mentioned in the chapter, Abraham and Rahab.(James2:18-25)

People have religious experiences of all sorts, whether they are saved or not. In churches emphasizing experience over objective truth, this is especially dangerous. Some individuals even have a superficial kind of repentance through which they liberate themselves from various vices. This is the case with the false prophets in 2 Peter 2. The chapter describes how these religious people infiltrate themselves into Christian assemblies and even occupy ministerial offices.

Peter tells us that they escaped the corruption of the world through the "knowledge" of Christ. Through this intellectual assent, they experienced a measure of deliverance. Yet they are "wells without water," born for destruction.

Outwardly, their profession may seem to be correct. Inwardly, they have "eyes full of adultery." They preach for money, and possess tremendous charm. They speak of "freedom," but are slaves of corruption.

Can The Regenerate Commit Serious Sin Or Fall Away Temporarily?

Absolutely! David fell into adultery and murder. This was a temporary fall, not a long-run lifestyle. God restored him. A believer committed incest in 1 Corinthians 5. Through church discipline, he was restored. Yes, Christians fall into sin. Even serious ones. A Christian in such a state may be indistinguishable from the lost. Sometimes only time will tell.

How Much Assurance Should Be Given To New Converts?

Modern evangelical culture has invented a series of repentance rituals that have nothing to do with salvation. Most of these are harmless, as long as no one gets the idea that they have anything to do with salvation. These little rituals include going forward at a meeting, praying a sinner's prayer, raising one's hand in meeting, etc.

Unfortunately, some groups give assurance based on the performance of these acts. Giving such assurance is unscriptural at best, and potentially dangerous, since none of these actions are the basis of salvation. They must *never* be presented as grounds for assurance of salvation. Doing so not only communicates a false gospel, but may give assurance to an unconverted individual.

It seems more advisable to proceed as did the Apostles.

First, they exhorted new converts to "continue in the faith." Then they taught them in their homes. During the studies, the rationale for a security of salvation became clear. Some receive assurance immediately from the Holy Spirit. For others, it comes slowly as they perceive God's grace working in their lives. We may give new converts assurance only when their lives show the characteristics of born again believers. This is the approach that John took. We must do the same.

Summary

The doctrine of preservation affirms that God has a people He preserves for heaven. Many Bible verses show that this doctrine can sustain itself without need of theological logic. Nevertheless, the theological arguments based on other doctrines would be sufficient to prove it even if such clear texts were absent. Intellectual honesty requires that preservation be given serious consideration.

Opponents to this doctrine invariably imagine that it grants to Christians a license to sin. The objection is self-contradictory, because sincere Christians do not want a license to sin. We have also shown that other views lead to a gospel of salvation by merits.

Preservation is, therefore, a gift of grace granted by God to His elect. The Christian is responsible for applying the means God has provided for his preservation. God Himself undertakes to ensure that the Elect do just that. The doctrine of preservation provides inestimable consolation for sincere Christians in their struggle against sin, giving them a substantial basis of security concerning the outcome.

Now to Him who is able to keep you from stumbling, And to present you faultless Before the presence of His glory with exceeding joy, To God our Savior, Who alone is wise, Be glory and majesty, Dominion and power,

Both now and forever. Amen. (Jude 24-25)

Objections

Though we dealt with the main objections in the chapter, certain ones are so common that they merit special treatment.

1. Hebrews 6:1-6 is the bulwark of the opponents of Preservation. They suppose it refers to backslidden Christians and shows that these have lost their salvation.

<u>Answer</u>

The most obvious problem with the above interpretation is that it proves more than the objectors intended. In verses 4 and 6, we read that those once enlightened cannot be restored to repentance. If the text refers to backslidden Christians, then we must declare it is impossible to restore a backslider. Few who base their views on this text are willing to affirm that. We all know Christians who have fallen away and later been restored. The Bible itself mentions examples. This alone is sufficient grounds to suspect that this text does not refer to backslidden Christians.

Objectors often give three reasons why they believe that Hebrews 6:1-6 refers to Christians: First, they claim that the doctrines mentioned here are uniquely Christian. Second, they claim that the spiritual experiences mentioned are distinctive to Christians, i.e., repentance, illumination by the Holy Spirit, and *tasting of the powers to come.* Third, they claim that the phrase *crucify again for themselves the Son of God* shows a knowledge of the Gospel. These three facts are supposed to be ample evidence that the lost individuals are those who were once born-again.

A careful reading of the entire chapter, along with

the previous one, reveals that the above presuppositions are groundless. First, it is untrue that the doctrines mentioned are uniquely Christian. They are typically Jewish also. The Old Testament teaches them all. Let's remember that Jesus taught nothing essentially new, but simply fulfilled things revealed before. These Judaic doctrines, therefore, were the foundation principles of His ministry.

Since these doctrines were also Jewish, no reason exists for assuming the "illumination" and "tasting" of the Spirit must refer to the born-again experience. The Jews had been "illuminated" by the Spirit through the Scriptures. They "tasted" the powers to come via the miracles and teachings of the prophets.

> *But, beloved, we are confident of better things concerning you, yes, things that accompany salvation, though we speak in this manner.* (Heb. 6:9)

Begining in verse 9, the author addresses a completely different audience than in the first part of the chapter. He calls this group *beloved,* a term never used in Scripture apart from God's people. He is *persuaded of better things* concerning them, as opposed to the curses of the people mentioned in verse 8. He considers them a people devoted to works of love in the name of Jesus, who minister to other believers. They are heirs of the covenant of Abraham, with a sure anchor for the soul. Nothing in verses 1-8 mentions anything like this. It is clear therefore, that the author is distinguishing between those saved and those merely religious.

As for the "knowledge" of the Gospel, nothing in the text proves that this was a *saving* knowledge. In summary, Hebrews 6 is not a contrast between backslidden Christians and faithful believers. It compares certain Jews who were vac-illating between Christianity and Judaism, with Jews committed to Christ. It is a warning to the indecisive to decide once and for all.

2.   Based on Galatians 5:4 (*You have become estranged from Christ, you who attempt to be justified by law; you have fallen from grace.*), opponents of preservation affirm that believers can fall from grace, lose their salvation, and be cut of from Christ.

Answer:
        Paul is warning the church as a whole of the danger of basing part of their salvation on anything other than Christ. He simply means that the church is in danger of apostatizing. He says nothing about individuals losing their salvation. Nor is there reason for interpreting the term 'fallen from grace' as equivalent to 'lose one's salvation.'Noewhere does Paul suggest that believers who fall into legalism have ceased to be Christians. He simply affirms they are inconsistent ones. Believers deprive themselves of the blessings of grace in their lives whenever they depend on law rather than the sufficiency of Christ. This is the point Paul is making to the church in Galatia.
        Further, Paul is warning the church as a whole of the danger of placing part of their justification on another basis than Christ. He simply means that the church as a whole is in danger of apostatizing. He says nothing about individuals losing their salvation.

3. The Doctrine of Preservation is contrary to the idea of free will.

Answer:
        The objection misunderstands free will. "Free" means the capacity to choose what one wants. What a person is,

determines what he wants. Since the will of a sinner is bound to his sinful nature, he rejects Christ. But the regenerate man chooses to persevere because he has a new nature. He *wants* to persevere. God does not have to force his will.

4. Preservation is a license to sin.

Answer:

Born-again people do not want a license to sin. The good news of preservation motivates them to purify themselves (1 John 3:3) Those who use the doctrine of preservation as a license to sin prove themselves to be reprobates.

5. Jesus said, *"He who perseveres to the end shall be saved."* This appears to contradict the doctrine of preservation.

Answer:

This objection reads several hidden presuppositions into the text. It assumes that some genuine believers do not persevere and thus are lost. Nothing in the text obliges us to assume that. It is true that those who persevere will be saved. It does not follow that some elect do not persevere.

Remember, a command to persevere proves only what we *ought* to do, not what we *can* do without grace. Such an objection would be as senseless as saying that faith is not a gift of God simply because God commanded, "Believe and you shall be saved."

6. In 1 Corinthians 9:27 Paul says, *"But I discipline my body and bring it into subjection, lest, when I have preached to others, I myself should become disqualified.* This text seems to express his concern about losing his salvation. How do we square this with preservation?

<u>Answer:</u>

Let's suppose that the term "disqualified" meant "lose salvation." This would not negate of preservation. It would simply show that Paul understood the importance of self-discipline as the means of preservation.

Nevertheless, it seems peculiar to affirm that the term "disqualified" can only mean "lose your salvation." If it can mean "disqualified" from ministry through lack of discipline, then no reason exists for assuming it must mean "lose your salvation."

Review Questions

1. The religious party in the 16th Century which taught that the regenerate can lose their salvation was called _____.

2. Our preservation is based primarily on two other doctrines. These are _____ and _____.

3. The basis of our preservation is in the will of _____ not the will of _____.

4. True or False: _____No condition exists by which a Christian could lose his salvation, even if he apostatized from the faith and lived a sinful life.

5. True or False: _____The doctrine of Preservation is a license to sin.

6. True or False: _____Since Preservation is by the grace of God, Christians are alleviated from all responsibility for applying the means of their preservation.

7. True or False: _____A problem with the doctrine of Preservation is that it deprives a person of free will.

8. Explain why Preservation is true if Election is true.

_____

_____

_____

9. Explain why Preservation is true if Justification is true.

_____

_____

_____

10. Explain why Preservation is true if God is sovereign.

_____

_____

_____

11. Explain why Preservation is true if the doctrine of the spiritual unity of the church is true._____

_____

_____

12. Explain why Preservation is true if the doctrine of Total Depravity is true._____

_____

_____

13. True or False: _____A significant aspect of Preservation is that God does not punish His people for their sins.

14. True or False: _____Those born of God do not practice a life of sin.

15. On the basis of 1Jn.5:18, explain why the regenerate do not practice a life of sin. _____

_____

_____

16. True or False: _____Hypothetically speaking, we can say that the soul of a backslidden Christian could end up in hell.

17. How do the regenerate act in view of the doctrine of Preservation? _____

18. Those who take advantage of the doctrine of Preservation to practice sin are_____ according to Jude 4.

19. The primary problem with the view that Christians can lose their salvation is_____

_____

20. True or False: _____The Bible teaches that believers can have security of salvation in this life.

21. True or False: _____Christ teaches that the elect are not able to be ultimately and finally deceived.

22. Explain how the intercession of Christ implies our preservation

_____

23. Explain the means that God uses to guarantee our preservation.

_____

24. True or False: _____A warning against the danger of falling away proves that some Christians have actually lost their salvation.

25. According to Mt.7:21-23, the condemned people mentioned in the text lack two things. These are:

    A._____

    B._____

26. True or False: _____An important element of the doctrine of Preservation is that a regenerate person can never commit a serious sin.

27. True or False: _____The doctrine of Preservation is so wonderful that it is wise to explain it to new converts as soon as they are converted.

28. True or False: _____It is possible that the basic doctrines referred to in Heb.6:1-3 refer to believers.

Notes:

1. This was the Arminian party, founded in Holland by the Dutch pastor Jacob Arminius, born 1560. The Synod of Dort in Holland debated his views in 1618 and proved them heretical.
2. Some groups of Baptists hold this view, and label it the doctrine of Eternal Security.
3. Throughout the remainder of this chapter, we shall use the term "Preservation" to distinguish the Reformed doctrine from the other two views.
4. The sense of the Greek verb requires this interpretation.
5. Note that 'work out' is not equivalent to 'work for'.

Chapter Summary — Security of the Believer

From this chapter on Preservation we learned that:

1. The question as to whether or not a Christian can lose his salvation depends on the nature of other doctrines such as Election and Justification. The conclusion is reached by reasonable and necessary deduction.
2. Genuine Christians do not desire a license to sin. Therefore, the accusation that this doctrine leads to a license to sin, is senseless.
3. Numerous Scriptures show that God preserves His people.
4. God preserves His people by numerous devices including exhortions, admonitions and fatherly chastisement. Ironically, He even uses our fear of falling as a device to preserve us.
5. Some people make professions of faith and persevere for a while, without ever having been regenerated. Even the Apostles could not tell the difference sometimes. We therefore must beware of judging others.

Chapter Eight

The Golden Chain
The Unity of the Doctrines of Grace in the Eternal Covenant

The Doctrines of Grace are like keys on a golden chain. We carry them to open our understanding of God's gracious purposes for us. What is this golden chain that binds them together? Let's call it the Covenant of Grace.

What Is A Covenant?

Covenant means "contract, agreement, or alliance." The Bible sometimes uses the word Testament as a synonym **for covenant**. Essentially a covenant means an agreement between two parties. When people make agreements, they do so because of expected mutual benefits in which each gives something to get something in return. The basis of all human contracts is this idea of mutual benefit.

In the Covenant of Grace, another principle dominates. God makes a covenant with man although man is unable to contribute anything. We have nothing to offer God in exchange for His grace. So the divine covenant has a unique character. It is more like an immutable decree in which all the benefits accrue to our side. The only benefit that God receives is the opportunity to display His grace and love.

How Was The Covenant Of Grace Instituted?

Sometimes the Covenant is called "Covenant With Abraham" because God instituted it with him. Although God manifested His grace beforehand in believers like Noah, Enoch and others, God declared it to Abraham in the formal sense of a legal covenant.

In Genesis 12, God spoke to Abraham about the fundamental nature of the covenant. Then in Genesis 17, He outlined some key elements. In verse 1, God reveals the basic condition: Walk with God and be perfect. Big problem! Nobody arrives at perfection in this life. Must we therefore wait until we get to heaven to enjoy the benefits of the covenant? Thanks to the imputed righteousness of Christ through justification, we experience the covenant benefits *now.*

Curiously, the covenant seems conditional and unconditional simultaneously, depending on the way we look at it. On one hand, it is conditional because God requires perfection. On the other, it is unconditional because Christ accomplished perfection for all the elect as their substitute.

God calls it *an everlasting covenant* in Genesis 17:7. Paul also, in Galatians 3, underlines the immutable character of the covenant by comparing it with human contracts. He argues that even if it were a mere human contract, no one annuls it or removes anything from it. How much more sure then, is a covenant made by God? *Brethren, I speak in the manner of men: Though it is only a man's covenant, yet if it is confirmed, no one annuls or adds to it* (v. 15). The Bible emphasizes the eternal character of the covenant in such texts as Isaiah 55:10; 59:21; 61:8-9; Galatians 3:6-15.

The Covenant includes believers *and* their children. God emphasizes this throughout Genesis 17. The point is supremely important because on the grounds of this principle we enter the covenant made with Abraham. Paul explains in Galatians 3-4 that Jesus Christ was the promised seed of Abraham. We also are Abraham's children through faith in Christ and participants in the same covenant.

Although the term "descendants" of Abraham has a figurative and spiritual aspect, it also contains a literal element. The offspring of believers enjoy certain advantages because of the covenant, although they may never be saved. The family element is central to the covenant.

This is notable in God's discourse with Abraham. In Genesis 17:18, Abraham said, *Oh, that Ishmael might live before You!* Abraham supposed that God was referring to Ishmael when he received the promise. But God explained that Sarah would give birth to another son, Isaac, who would be the real heir of the covenant. Nevertheless, God blessed Ishmael also with earthly blessings, simply because Ishmael was a child of Abraham.

The Bible abounds in precious promises regarding the children of the righteous:

> *"As for Me," says the Lord, "this is My covenant with them: My Spirit who is upon you, and My words which I have put in your mouth, shall not depart from your mouth, nor from the mouth of your descendants, nor from the mouth of your descendants' descendants," says the Lord, "from this time and forevermore."* (Isaiah 59:21)

The offspring of the righteous will not lack food (Psalm 37:25). They will live securely (Psalm 102:28). They will have hope (Proverbs 14:26) They will be blessed (Proverbs 20:7).

The Apostles recognized this family aspect of the Covenant. Peter declared in his sermon at Pentecost: *For the promise is to you and to your children, and to all who are afar off, as many as the Lord our God will call.* (Acts 2:39) Paul recognized a certain legal sanctification (although not regenerative) on the families of believers in 1 Corinthians 7:14: *For the unbelieving husband is sanctified by the wife, and the unbelieving wife is sanctified by the husband; otherwise your children would be unclean, but now they are holy.*

The Sign and Seal Of The Covenant

God gave circumcision to Abraham as the external sign of the covenant (Genesis 17:10; Romans 4:11) This sign was to continue until Jesus came and changed it to baptism (Colossians 2:11-12). The two signs symbolize the same thing: The change of heart that God gives to His people (Romans 2:28 29 with Titus 3:5-6). The word "sign" means "symbol" and suggests the relationship of the believer to the covenant. The word "seal" indicates the divine promise to fulfill the benefits of the covenant.

What Are The Benefits Of The Covenant?

A story is told about a poor man from Europe who wanted to immigrate to the United States to have a better life. He had barely enough money for the ticket on the ship, but not enough for food for the trip. He bought the ticket, and boarded the ship with the little food he had – a loaf of bread and a chunk of cheese. He hoped that this food would last until he arrived in New York.

For three weeks this gentleman lived on his bread and cheese, avoiding the dining room where it pained him to see the other passengers enjoying the sumptuous dishes. On the last day of the trip, he happened to notice something written on the back of his ticket: "All meals are included."

The covenant of grace is like the ticket of the poor passenger. Some Christians live deprived of the promised benefits, because they fail to understand what their "ticket" includes. Their prayers take the character of pleadings like beggars, not a solid faith, because they do not understand their rights under the covenant.

Let's Take A Look At Some Of The Covenant Promises

A. The Promise of the Holy Spirit

    In Galatians 3:14 we read *"that the blessing of Abraham might come upon the Gentiles in Christ Jesus, that we might receive the promise of the Spirit through faith."*
Christ died on the cross, according to verse 13, to guarantee that the power of the Spirit would reach all believers, Jews and gentiles. This includes all the Spirit's ministries: His power, His gifts, His work of sanctification and liberation in the life of the believer.

    The devil assails believers, trying to give them an inferiority complex. To the women he says, "You can't have the power of the Spirit, nor spiritual gifts, because you are only a woman." To the men he says, "That's for women." To the youth he says, "You're too young. You need more maturity to be blessed with spiritual gifts." To the elders he says, "You're too old. The young people won't listen to you." The promise of the Spirit is for *all* of Abraham's children.

    At Pentecost, Peter said that God would pour out His Spirit on all flesh: *And it shall come to pass in the last days, says God, That I will pour out of My Spirit on all flesh; Your sons and your daughters shall prophesy, Your young men shall see visions, Your old men shall dream dreams (Acts 2:17).*

    We pray with more confidence as we understand why God is willing to grant us His power and His gifts. Our ticket, the covenant of grace, includes all these.

B. Blessings On Our Children

    The Devil lies to parents, telling them that it is scarcely worth while to pray for their wayward children because after all, the children have free will. God would hardly see fit to violate *that*. God never asked Isaac's permission before declaring him as heir of the covenant. The Lord promises blessing on the children of believers simply because they are children of believers – not because they have a cooperative free will. God has more regard for His covenant than He does for the state of their will.

The covenant of grace gives Christian parents a solid basis for praying for their children. Satan cannot prevent God from blessing their children because the grounds of such blessings is His covenant, not the will of the children.

C. An Eternal Inheritance

According to Hebrews 9:15, Christ died to guaranteed that the called of God would attain their eternal inheritance: *And for this reason He is the Mediator of the new covenant, by means of death, for the redemption of the transgressions under the first covenant, that those who are called may receive the promise of the eternal inheritance.*

Christians occasionally become discouraged when they consider their faults and weaknesses. It seems impossible to attain to the entire perfection that the Bible promises. The struggle against sin appears so difficult. But we have a covenant with God, along with a Guarantor who guarantees the victory. *He who calls you is faithful, who also will do it. (1 Thessalonians 5:24).*

D. Victory Over Our Enemies

God promised Abraham, *I will bless those who bless you, And I will curse him who curses you; And in you all the families of the earth shall be blessed* (Genesis 12:3). Zacharias, father of John the Baptist, prayed: *That we should be saved from our enemies And from the hand of all who hate us,*

To perform the mercy promised to our fathers And to remember His holy covenant,

The oath which He swore to our father Abraham:
To grant us that we, Being delivered from the hand of our enemies,
Might serve Him without fear,
In holiness and righteousness before Him all the days of our life.
"And you, child, will be called the prophet of the Highest; For you
will go before the face of the Lord to prepare His ways,
Luke 1:71-75

God has surprising methods for liberating us from our enemies. Sometimes He converts them to Christ! Although Christians receive persecution, they know that God has even this under His control and even this will help the furtherance of the Gospel. Paul recognized this by saying, *For we can do nothing against the truth, but for the truth. 2Cor.13:8*

The Acronym "Si, Jesus," and the Doctrines of Grace

These doctrines are really component elements of the covenant of grace. Let's examine each of these to see how they relate.

A. Sovereignty of God

The covenant is based directly on the immutability of the sovereign will of God. In the first chapter, we saw that nothing in God changes including His eternal attributes. All His counsels are irresistible.

Few other Bible texts shed more light on the link between the covenant and God's immutable will than Hebrews 6:13-20. In ancient times, people sealed covenants with oaths. God accommodated Himself to this custom by inaugurating the covenant with an oath: *For when God made a promise to Abraham, because He could swear by no one greater, He swore by Himself, saying, "Surely blessing I will bless you, and multiplying I will multiply you....Thus God, determining to show more abundantly to the heirs of promise the immutability of His counsel, confirmed it by an oath."* (Hebews 6:13-14, 17)

In thinking about our relationship to God within the covenant, it helps to remember that the divine decrees are immutable. This alleviates the fear that God may remove us from the covenant for our faults. God helps us set aside such notions by basing the covenant in His own character via an oath.

B. Inability of Man

The nation of Israel had nothing to offer when God established the covenant. Through Ezekiel, God said in a parable, *And when I passed by you and saw you struggling in your own blood, I said to you in your blood, "Live!" Yes, I said to you in your blood, "Live!"* (16:6). Israel was like a newborn child, abandoned. Only death awaited her. But God, like a rich and compassionate man, took Israel and adopted her as his own child.

We also were born dead in sin, insensible to divine things, selfish and insensitive. Nevertheless, God bound us to Himself with a covenant. In this doctrine of total inability we see the unconditional aspect of the covenant. We contributed nothing.

C. Justification by Faith

Abraham faced a terrible dilemma when God told him, *walk before Me and be blameless. And I will make My covenant between Me and you."* (Genesis 17:2-3*)*. How discouraging to hear that perfection is the condition for having the benefits of the covenant! That is enough to dishearten the most saintly because nobody is perfect. Is there a solution?

Yes! Jesus Christ! He is the only one who fulfilled the condition necessary to obtain the benefits of the covenant. But since we are in Christ, we have in Him all the benefits through faith. *And the glory which You gave Me I have given them, that they may be one just as We are one* (John 17:22).

D. Election By Grace

Election proceeds from the covenant since God accomplished it for His elect only. *I have made a covenant with My chosen* (Psalm 89:3) He never made a covenant like this with any other nation but Israel because it was the only elect nation. The Covenant is particular, not universal.

E. Sacrifice of Christ

The Cross bought something for Christ, also. It purchased the right to act as Guarantor, High Priest and Mediator of the covenant. (Hebrews 7:22 and Chapters 8, 9 & 10 of Hebrews.) A guarantor is a person with the authority to ensure that the participants in an agreement receive the benefits promised. *By so much more Jesus has become a surety of a better covenant* (Hebrews 7:22).

When God gave Moses the Law, he sprinkled with blood the books, the Ark of Testimony, and the other elements of the service, as a sign of the confirmation of the covenant (Hebrews 8-9).
The same principle of confirmation by blood exists in the covenant of grace. The blood of Christ is God's final confirmation of the covenant.

F. Universality of the Church and Spiritual Unity of All Believers

The people of God in both Testaments, Old and New, are bound together by the same covenantal relationship. There exists only one people of God, not two. As Paul showed through the example with Abraham, the Old Testament saints were saved in essentially the same manner as we. They were justified by faith, had the same Savior, and participated in the same covenant. Paul even called this covenant, "the good news, i.e., the Gospel (Galatians 3:8).

The Lord's Supper illustrates the covenant bond between God and His people as His people participate together in it. Jesus said,

> *"Take, eat; this is My body." Then He took the cup, and gave thanks, and gave it to them, saying, "Drink from it, all of you. For this is My blood of the new covenant, which is shed for many for the remission of sins." (Matt. 26:26-28).*

Paul depicted the same in 1 Corinthians 10:17, by comparing the bread of the Supper with us, the Church. *For we, though many, are one bread and one body; for we all partake of that one bread.* Though the bread represents Christ primarily, it also symbolizes the spiritual unity we have with each other in Christ.

G. Security of the Elect

The immutability of the covenant, the efficacy of the ministry of the Lord Jesus as Mediator, the imputation of the righteousness of Christ, the efficacy of His sacrifice to confirm the Covenant – all these elements of the covenant make up the security of the Elect. God chastises His children as proof that they belong to Him and that He will never abandon them (Hebrews 12:6-10).

From the viewpoint of pure justice, there seems no good reason for the Jews to exist today. Where are the Edomites, the Philistines, the Gibeonites? Extinct races all. The only explanation is, *For I am the Lord, I do not change; There-fore you are not consumed, O sons of Jacob* (Malachi 3:6). Though God destroyed other nations for committing the same sins as Israel, yet God preserved His Elect nation. *But the Lord was gracious to them, had compassion on them, and regarded them, because of His covenant with Abraham, Isaac, and Jacob, and would not yet destroy them or cast them from His presence (2 Kings 13:23).*

The inexpressible comfort of the covenant resides in that, "The bond of the covenant is capable of carrying the weight of the believer's heaviest burden."[1] Though God punishes and corrects His elect people and causes them to grieve over their sins, He never casts them away. *I say then, has God cast away His people? Certainly not! For I also am an Israelite, of the seed of Abraham, of the tribe of Benjamin. God has not cast away His people whom He foreknew* (Romans 11:1-2).

Let no one imagine that our participation in the covenant relieves us from participating in corrective disciplines. To the contrary, it is precisely because of the covenant that God corrects His children. *You only have I known of all the families of the earth; Therefore I will punish you for all your iniquities* (Amos 3:2).

The covenant is a paradox. It is both a profound security and a serious warning. It guarantees an eternal inheritance, but promises no easy roads . . . just a sure destination. The covenant is an uncomfortable security, in which God spares nothing to ensure our maturity and obedience.

Summary

By the sovereign will of God, the elect have an inviolable agreement with God, with the guarantee of an eternal inheritance. It includes promises for their children, victory over enemies, and provision for their needs. Though the elect are entirely incapable and totally unworthy to enter the covenant, Christ died to confirm the covenant. By the gift of faith, He justifies them, so as to unite them with the people of God of every epoch. He is forming them into one body with Christ, saved and kept forever. *This hope we have as an anchor of the soul, both sure and steadfast, and which enters the Presence behind the veil* (Hebrews 6:19).

Review Questions

1. The covenant of grace differs from human contracts in that:
   A. God makes covenants only with those who do good works.
   B. Man contributes nothing to the covenant.
   C. The covenant of grace was never put in writing.

2. Sometimes the covenant of grace is called
   _____.

3. True or False_____ Before the covenant with Abraham, grace did not exist.

4. True or False_____ The covenant is conditional and unconditional simultaneously, according to our perspective.

5. True or False_____ God requires perfection as a condition of the covenant.

6. When God makes a covenant with a believer, He also includes_____.

7. God gave to Abraham the rite of _____ as an external sign of the covenant. But in the New Testament changes this sign to _____.

8. The benefits of the covenant are:
   A.
   B.
   C.
   D.

9. The covenant of grace is a solid basis for our
_____ of salvation.

10. The doctrine of the sovereignty of God relates to the covenant of grace in that,

11. The doctrine of the total inability of man relates to the covenant of grace in that,

12. The doctrine of Justification relates to the covenant of grace in that,

13. The doctrine of Election relates to the covenant of grace in that,

14. The doctrine of the sacrifice of Christ relates to the covenant of grace in that,

15. The doctrine of the universality and unity of all believers relates to the covenant of grace in that,

16. The doctrine of the security of the elect relates to the covenant of grace in that,

17. True or False_____ God promises to destroy completely our disobedient children if they do not fulfill the requirements of the covenant.

18. True or False_____ Our participation in the covenant relieves us from all divine corrections for our sins.

Notes:

1. William S. Plumer, *Gathered Gold*, John Blanchaard, pp. 52

Chapter Summary — The Golden Chain
From this chapter on the Covenant of Grace we learned that:

1. The Bible covenant of grace conditional in the sense that God requires perfection as the condition to enter into it. It is unconditional in the sense that God Himself fulfills that condition through the perfect sacrifice of Christ.
2. The doctrines of grace are actually component parts and benefits of the covenant.
3. The divine promises of salvation and all the benefits thereof are actually covenant promises.
4. Benefits of the covenant include the promise of the Holy Spirit, blessings on our children, eternal inheritance and victory over our enemies.

Epilogue
Grace Wants to Go Home

Occasionally someone asks me why I wrote this book. I experience a twinge of chagrin at this because I suspect that the reader has missed something in the message of grace. Grace is restless. Assuming it is real, it cannot stay put and do nothing. It wants to go places and do things. The thing it most wants to do is glorify God. The place it most wants to go is back home. Those of us who have received a genuine portion of grace know this. And each of us, in his own distinctive way, will feel compelled to give something back in gratitude. If we do not feel this, we may rightly doubt if our portion was real.

What parent has not had a child hand a gift to him which came from the parent in the first place? The difference with grace, though, is that when we give it back, we find it still in our hand, but altered. It has grown bigger. It wants to return to its Source so as to be more than it was before. I am a writer. I do not know how else to give back my portion. So I wrote this book for the simplest of reasons.
I wrote it because I could not do otherwise

Appendix A
Answers to Review Questions

Introduction
1. grace, 2. the doctrines of grace, 3. F, 4. master, fate, 5. F, 6. controlling everything, 7. T, 8. before the creation of the world, 9. all of them, 10. salvation, 11. F, 12. God, 13. Adam, 14. F, 15. righteousness of Christ, 16. no, 17. Christ, 18. attributed, righteousness, 19. declared just, 20. F, 21. T, 22. dead, 23. the Cross, 24. possibility, accomplished, 25. F.

Chapter One
1. The sovereignty of God, 2. human, 3. the sovereignty of God, 4. it is shipwrecked, crumbles, 5. divine decrees, 6. bad, sovereignty, 7. F, 8. will, 9. sovereign, 10. F, 11. F, 12. T, 13. the sovereignty of God, 14. all, 15. no, 16. because He does not deserve all the glory, 17. controlling everything, 18. man, honor, 19. F.

Foundations of this Doctrine: 1. a. His attributes of omnipotence and omniscience, b. His immutable will, c. the derivation of reality from His will, d. God's sovereign ownership **of** everything, 2. knows everything, 3. all powerful, 4. omniscience and omnipresence, 5. immutable, 6. irresistible, 7. T, 8. resist, 9. F, 10. yes, 11. see text, 12. the divine decrees, 13. the decreed will of God, 14. F, 15

Chapter Two
1. Moral Free Will; 2. Gospel; 3. F; 4. T; 5. T; 6. Free Will; 7. Total Inability; 8. F;
9. A. Destroys pride, B. Gives Security; 10. His entire being became enslaved to sin; 11. His descendants; 12. A; 13. B;

14. A; 15. F; 16. Responsibility, Ability; 17. B; 18. (See text of book); 19. Knowledge

Chapter Three
1. T; 2. F; 3. F; 4. F; 5: T; 6. F; 7. T; 8. F; 9. F; 10. F; 11. justification; by faith 12. Martin Luther; 13. Freedom from fear; relating to the Father better; avoiding legalism; 14. life, death 15. F; 16. T; 17. a righteous life

Chapter Four
1. B; 2. Foreordained; 3. Divine decree to chose some for salvation; 4. T; 5. T; 6. Objection on the grounds of concept of justice and objection on the grounds of foreknowledge; 7. Romans 9; 8. That is not fair!; 9.C; 10. Arguing with God; 11. Mercy, justice, injustice; 12. Know beforehand; 13. faith, good works, good will; 14. Fore-ordained; 15. F; 16. Omniscient; 17. Jacob & Esau; Pharaoh; potter & clay; 18. F; 19.   Nations are made up of individuals; The context refers to individuals; 20. elect, reprobate; 21. F; 22. T; 23. particular, universal; 24. v. 16; 25. reprobation; 26. see text; 27. F; 28. God's justice, God's mercy; 29. F; 30. A; 31. holiness, love, adoption, redemption, sealed (See Ephesians 1.); 32. Refers to the plan of God to include the Gentiles; They claim that the phrase "in Christ" means that God foresees that we were going to accept Christ; 33. F; 34. F; 35. C; 36. T; 37. F; 38. B; 39. F; 40. F

Chapter Five
1. F; 2. Particular Redemption; Universal Atonement; 3. B; 4. A; 5. See text; 6. F; 7. Sheep;   8. Gave His life for them; 9. T; 10. F; 11. C; 12. "Those the Father has given Me"; 13. T; 14. First, we belong to God by divine decree before belonging to Christ; Second, all those that the Father gave to Him, will come to Christ; Third, the will of God determines everything;

15. total human inability; effectual call; sovereign regeneration; security of the elect; 16. Chapter 17; 17. Those the Father gave Him; 18. A; 19. B; 20. Those for whom Christ died could be condemned; 21. B; 22. F; 23. election, covenant, sacrifice; 24. the called; 25. A. Sacrifice, B. Intercession; 26. T; 27. F; 28. A. His people, B. the sheep, C. His Church, D. the called, E. those the Father gave Him; 29. All will be saved; 30. B; 31. appease wrath; 32. B; 33. F; 34. B; 35. T

Chapter Six
1. F; 2. T; 3. F; 4. T; 5. T; 6. F; 7. T; 8. F; 9. F; 10. F; 11. Doctrine, Organization, Testimony, Worship; 12. T; 13. F; 14. T; 15. T; 16. F; 17. F; 18. F; 19. F; 20. F

Chapter Seven
1.Arminian; 2.Justification;Election; 3.God, Man; 4.F; 5.F; 6.F; 7.F; 8,9,10,11&12.See Text; 13.F; 14.T; 15.See Text; 16.T; 17.It inspires them to purify themselves, IJn.3:3; 18.Reprobate; 19.Supposes that salvation is a cooperative work between God and man.; 20.T; 21.T; 22.God always answers theprayers of Christ. Therefore, the prayers of Christ for our preservation are answered.; 23.Fear of God, exhortations, threats, warnings.; 24.F; 25. Do God's will and live a holy life; 26.F; 27.F; 28.F

Chapter Eight
1. B; 2. Covenant with Abraham; 3. F; 4. T; 5. T; 6. their children; 7. circumcision; baptism; 8. A) Holy Spirit, B) Blessing on the children C)Justification D)Eternal Inheritance; 9. Security; 10. believers of all ages participate in it ; 11. man contributes nothing to the covenant; 12. Christ accomplished the requirement of perfection under the covenant as our substitute; 13. The covenant is for the elect only; 14. The blood

of Christ confirms the covenant, making Christ the Guarantor and Mediator of it; 15.Via the Covenant, there exists only one people of God; 16. The covenant is the grounds of our security of salvation; 17. F; 18. F

Available from Deo Volente Publishing

Faith at Work: Studies in the Book of James by Carol Ruvolo, ISBN#0-9658804-3-5, Trade paperback, 400 pp, $14.95

Footprints of the Fisherman: Life Lessons From One Who Walked Closely With Christ by Carol Ruvolo, ISBN#0-9658804-7-8 Trade paperback, 248 pp, $10.95

God Speaks: what the Bible Teaches About Itself by Dr. R. Will Butler, ISBN#0-9658804-4-3, Trade paperback, 87 pp, $6.95

Plain Talk About Genesis by Dr. John Reed, ISBN#0-9658804-6-X Trade paperback, 119 pp, $9.95

Prowl (Christian action, adventure) by Gordan Runyan, ISBN#0-9658804-5-1, Trade paperback, 296 pp, $12.95

Unlocking Grace: A Study Guide in the Doctrines of Grace by Roger Smalling, ISBN#0-9658804-8-6, Trade paperback, 180 pp, $10.95

¡Si, Jesus! (Spanish version of *Unlocking Grace*) by Roger Smalling, ISBN#958-9269-85-0, Trade paperback, 178 pp, $7.95

To Order:
Call: 866-672-1622 Toll Free
FAX: 505-672-1615
Web: www.deovolente.net

Ask about discounts for retailers and study groups.

DEO VOLENTE
PUBLISHING
P.O. BOX 4847
LOS ALAMOS, NM 87544